SHAMBHALA DRAGON EDITIONS

The dragon is an age-old symbol of the highest spiritual essence, embodying wisdom, strength, and the divine power of transformation. In this spirit, Shambhala Dragon Editions offers a treasury of readings in the sacred knowledge of Asia. In presenting the works of authors both ancient and modern, we seek to make these teachings accessible to lovers of wisdom everywhere.

Each Shambhala Dragon Edition features Smyth-sewn binding and is printed on acid-free paper.

Dr. Daisetz Teitaro Suzuki in London, 1954

# The Awakening
# of Zen

DAISETZ TEITARO SUZUKI

*Edited by Christmas Humphreys*

**SHAMBHALA**
*Boston & London*
1987

Shambhala Publications, Inc.
Horticultural Hall
300 Massachusetts Avenue
Boston, Massachusetts 02115

*In association with*
The Buddhist Society
58 Eccleston Square
London, SW1 1PH

9 8 7 6 5 4 3 2 1

FIRST SHAMBHALA EDITION
Printed in the United States of America
Distributed in the United States by Random House
and in Canada by Random House of Canada Ltd.

Library of Congress Cataloging-in-Publication Data
Suzuki, Diasetz Teitaro, 1870–1966.
   The awakening of Zen.
   Reprint. Originally published: Boulder, Colo.:
Prajña Press, 1980.
   "Shambhala dragon editions."
   1. Zen Buddhism. I. Humphreys, Christmas, 1901–
II. Title.
[BQ9266.S94 1987]   294.3'927      87-9656
ISBN 0-87773-423-2 (pbk.)

# Contents

# FOREWORD

In the course of his very long life Dr. D. T. Suzuki wrote and lectured enormously on the subject of Zen Buddhism. His works total some fifty books in Japanese and English, a wide variety of articles and essays for numerous publications and lectures, formal and informal, which were taken down and transcribed.

When, in 1946, I returned from a visit to Japan, where I had been able to spend much time with him, I was appointed his agent for works published in Europe. I arranged with Rider and Co. to publish and republish them as they appeared, and for many years kept them in print, in some cases with American editions and foreign translations.

But I soon possessed material for a further volume of lectures and articles from various sources, and published them through Rider and Co. as *Studies in Zen* (1955). Years later I had sufficient material to rescue from oblivion a further selection which the Buddhist Society published as *The Field of Zen* (1969), and this was followed in 1971 by *What is Zen*, containing two articles acquired by Mr. Lunsford Yandell and a reprint of *The Essence of Buddhism*, being the two lectures to the Emperor of Japan, first published in 1946.

Articles and lectures continued to be added to my files. I noted the series of posthumous essays published in the last few years in *The Eastern Buddhist*, and am happy to learn that they will, before long, be published in volume form, but many more have appeared in journals such as the Buddhist Society's *The Middle Way*, and these would be lost to the general public unless collected in book form. Hence the present volume, containing items extremely varied in nature.

In Dr. Suzuki's writings in English there seem to be at least four types of style and purpose. The first is scholarship, in which he adds to the world's knowledge of the history of Ch'an (in Japanese, Zen) Buddhism, and the meaning of the recorded sayings of Masters which constitute its scriptures. Then there are those occasions where he is transmitting, if the term has meaning, the "Zen" of the Rinzai School, and its methods of achieving this state of consciousness for those with minds capable of receiving it at a high intellectual level. Thirdly, there are articles and lectures pitched in a lower key, to help those of humbler capacity to gain at least some idea of "what it's all about." Finally, there are comparisons of Zen with other fields of enquiry, as with Jung's psychology. All are represented in this voume, but it is not for the Editor to suggest into what category any one item should be placed.

The author himself had clearly achieved a very highly developed intuition, which is the level of consciousness on which Zen "functions," and he would speak, impromptu if need be, to a meeting large or small from that level, choosing his words according to the needs and ability of his audience. Hence, as many have found, although one may read numerous books and articles in which he tried to convey the spirit of Zen to a Western audience, there may be in one more talk or lecture that sudden spark from mind to mind which lights up the reader's ignorance, as nothing has before. Sooner or later the last word of transmission from this profoundly illumined mind should be recovered and preserved. Here at least is further material. While planning the volume I had the good fortune to meet again Mr. Samuel Bercholz of Shambhala Publications, Inc. of the United States of America, and he at once suggested joint publication with the Buddhist Society, an offer gladly accepted.

Little difficulty arises in the matter of copyright, especially when all the material came into being at least twenty years ago. I have done what I can to obtain permission to reprint articles from magazines but find that several have ceased to exist. As for the talks, many were given at or under the auspices of the Buddhist Society, or on occasions where it has proved impossible to trace the organizer of the meeting at which they were given. I apologize to those, if any, to whom I seem to have been discourteous.

The material in this volume covers a wide field, from that of Mahāyāna Buddhism generally to the Zen school of Buddhism in particular; from Japanese art and culture to the first translation into English of a sermon from the "Sayings of Rinzai"; from formal lectures to informal talks to an enraptured audience at the Buddhist Society; from Zen Buddhism and its relation to Western psychology to the famous lecture at the Queen's Hall in London in 1936 on "The Supreme Spiritual Ideal," which none of us present will forget.

An adequate biography of this famous and deeply spiritual man has yet to be written, but as most of the material in this volume appeared on visits to Europe I have added part of the report on the Centenary of his birth as celebrated at the Buddhist Society in London in October 1970.

# Dr. D. T. Suzuki

## (October 18, 1870–1970)

The Lecture Hall was crowded on October 21st last to commemo-
rate the Centenary of the birth of Dr. D. T. Suzuki whom the
President, in the Chair, described in terms of spiritual grandeur as the
greatest man he had met. He reminded the audience of this great
scholar-sage's life, from his birth in Kanazawa of a long line of
doctors, through his early education to the time when, abandoning
his university career to sit at the feet, first of Kosen Imagita Roshi and
then Soyen Shaku Roshi in Engakuji, Kamakura, he broke through
the veils of thought, and achieved his enlightenment.

Mr. Humphreys read from the chapter in *The Field of Zen* in which
Dr. Suzuki gives his own description of this, the greatest event in his
long and fruitful life. He agreed to help Dr. Paul Carus in Chicago in
his Buddhist writings, and knew that the time was short to achieve his
"break-through." His master had given him the koan "Mu," and the
winter *sesshin* of December 1896 might be his last chance. As he
wrote in "Early Memories," "I must have put all my spiritual strength
into that sesshin. Up till then I had always been conscious that Mu
was in my mind. But so long as I was conscious of Mu it meant that
somehow I was separate from Mu, and that is not a true *samādhi*. But
about the fifth day I ceased to be conscious of Mu. I was one with Mu,
identified with Mu, so that there was no longer the separateness
implied by being conscious of Mu. This is the real state of *Samādhi*.

"But this *Samādhi* alone is not enough. You must come out of that
state, be awakened from it, and that awakening is *Prajñā*. That
moment of coming out of *Samādhi,* and seeing it for what it is, *that* is
*satori*. When I came out of that state of *Samādhi* I said, 'I see. This is
it.'"

x

*Satori*

The next day his master approved his *satori,* and he concludes, "I remember that night as I walked back from the monastery seeing the trees in the moonlight. They looked transparent, and I was transparent too."

It must have been at this time, said Mr. Humphreys, that his master gave him his Buddhist name of Daisetz, "great humility."

Thereafter the speaker told of his long sojourn in the U.S.A. and of his first visit to England in 1912, when he took part in the work of the original Buddhist Society of Great Britain and Ireland. In 1921, back in Japan, he founded *The Eastern Buddhist* and remained its Editor for the next thirty years. In 1927 London received the first series of his *Essays in Zen Buddhism*, which opened the eyes of English Buddhists to the range and glory of the Mahāyāna and in particular to the direct school of Rinzai Zen. Further volumes followed, and in 1938 Dr. Suzuki wrote a foreword to his wife's book *Mahāyāna Buddhism* which she kindly wrote for the Society. Meanwhile, for his famous two volumes on the Laṅkāvatāra Sūtra and Commentary upon it he was given an Hon. D. Litt. by Otani University, Kyoto. In later life he was more fully honored with membership of the Japanese Academy and the Cultural Medal presented to him by the Emperor.

But Mr. Humphreys was mainly concerned with Dr. Suzuki's connection with the Society, the first occasion being in 1936 when he came to Europe for a lecture tour, and to attend the London meeting of the World Congress of Faiths. The speaker described his memorable speech at the Queen's Hall on the set subject of the Supreme Spiritual Ideal. It seemed that Dr. Suzuki had to be woken up to give his contribution, but then, brushing aside the given theme, which he said he did not understand, he spoke of his "little thatched house" in Japan, and thus brought the vast audience down to the realities of Zen which are to be found in matters here and now rather than in abstract phrases.

When he paid his first visit to the Society, on 20th July 1936, he proved himself, said the speaker, a real Zen master. Quoting from Alan Watts's recollection of that memorable evening, which tallied with his own diary, he said,

"A member of the audience asked him, 'Dr. Suzuki, when you use the word reality, are you referring to the relative reality of the physical world or to the absolute reality of the transcendental world?'

He closed his eyes and went into that characteristic attitude which some of us called 'doing a Suzuki,' for no one could tell whether he was in deep meditation or fast asleep. After about a minute's silence he opened his eyes and said, 'Yes.'"

Dr. Suzuki spent the war in seclusion, writing in English and Japanese, suspect for his Western sympathies. "In 1946," said Mr. Humphreys, "I went to Japan for some seven months as a lawyer concerned in the International Trials. I spent my days in my office, and my evenings and weekends working for Japanese Buddhism. I was not troubled by this dichotomy—nor were the Japanese. I found Dr. Suzuki in his 'little thatched house' in Kamakura and he was delighted indeed to renew his contact with the West. I took down in long-hand his translation of the two lectures which he gave to the Emperor on Japanese Buddhism, which we published in London as *The Essence of Buddhism,* and took possession of the commentary on the Sutra of Hui Neng which we published in London as *The Zen Doctrine of No-Mind.* I noted the profound respect in which he was held in all monasteries, although of course he was not a monk, much less a great Abbot. He was busy founding the Matsugoaka Library with his own books and those of the late Mrs. Suzuki. He taught me in one remark what Zen is not, and gave a hint of what it is. We were discussing Buddhism as pantheism. 'I see what you mean,' I said, 'all is God but there is no God.' 'No,' he said, after the usual moment's thought. 'It would be better to say, "All is God and there is no God."' You must work that one out," said Mr. Humphreys to his puzzled audience, "for yourselves."

The speaker then described how Dr. Suzuki made him his London agent and how, with the help of Rider and Co., some eight volumes of the Collected Works in English were rapidly published.

"In 1953," said Mr. Humphreys, "he came to London again, this time with Miss Mihoko Okamura, his lovely and charming secretary-companion who gave her life to the old gentleman—he was already eighty-three—for the next twelve years." Quoting from a report in *The Middle Way* of Dr. Suzuki's attendance at the Annual General Meeting he read, "We noted he was one of the few who could lift the audience for the time being beyond the limitation of concept, and enable them to share what was to him a living and immediate experience."

"He came again in 1954, but his longest stay was in 1958, and we made the most of him. He arrived in time for Wesak, with a full program of lectures and visits already planned. We claimed every moment of his spare time, and although then eighty-eight he gave us lectures, attended classes, and meetings at members' homes, and we took him sight-seeing. He possessed the most dreadful old umbrella, but finally allowed us to substitute a new one, and to place the old one, as it is here tonight, on the mantelpiece for meetings of what was immediately called 'The Brolly Club.' His sense of humor was so deep-grained that somehow a large part of our time with him was taken up with laughter. Writing on his bed in the Rembrandt Hotel he gave us six most beautiful specimens of his handwriting.

"But all things have an end, and in time we had to say good-bye. Even at the airport he was helping me to understand a point made on the previous evening, on the relation of the unconscious to *satori,* and as he demonstrated what he meant with a diagram on the back of an envelope, for the moment I understood. Then he went away.

"I continued a long correspondence with him, and he was most generous in help on the precise meaning of Japanese terms in my *Popular Dictionary of Buddhism.* He promised to bequeath us one half of the royalties I collected on some of the books we published in London, but in 1965 most generously gave us there and then one half of the sum already collected, some £1,800.

"A year later he was taken ill, just before, at the age of 95, leaving for a summer holiday on which he proposed to read proofs, finish a book and write an Introduction to another. He died on 12th July 1966. As was written by Sohaku Kobori Roshi in the Memorial issue of *The Eastern Buddhist:*

On the afternoon of 14th July, his body became a wreath of white smoke in the crematorium in Kita Kamakura. The smoke vanished into the cool breeze blowing from the sea. Where did he go? Look, here he is. He will never die—the vow he made! His great will, which communicated the incommunicable, and shared it with all human beings, will not vanish forever. The wheel of this vow, which had gone throughout his 95 years, must be driven further and further, generation after generation, as long as human beings exist on the earth.

"He was," continued Mr. Humphreys, "a Zen man, a man of Zen. Of Westerners I only knew R. H. Blyth and Father Thomas Merton

who seemed to speak with even comparable authority. His appeal
was that of Bodhidharma, Hui Neng, Huang Po and Rinzai himself,
to direct enlightenment, where the Wisdom of *Prajñā* is merged in
ceaseless action in the service of mankind. He was in the direct line of
the great masters, and spoke and wrote from their awareness. He
lived in the Wisdom with a truly divine compassion for all living
things.

"In fifty years of work in the field of Buddhism I have known great
men and women of many nationalities. I have met and studied with
great Theras of the Theravada, great Lamas of Tibet, great Roshis of
Japan, but all in all I have met none with the sheer spiritual grandeur
of Daisetz Teitaro Suzuki."

The Chairman then called on Dr. Carmen Blacker, Reader in
Japanese in Cambridge University, who had worked with Miss
Okamura to obtain from Dr. Suzuki the material which now appears
under "Early Memories" in *The Field of Zen.* Dr. Blacker gave a most
vivid description of personal visits to Dr. Suzuki and his secretary
companion, Miss Mihoko Okamura. She asked him if he would give
an account of his first contacts with Zen, and she wrote down his
description, as he gave it, in his little house on the hillside, looking
across the valley to the roofs of the Engakuji Monastery.

Dr. Suzuki described visits to Zen masters, and the harsh, tough
treatment he had endured. She was struck by the mind which had
responded to the koan training, and his treatment had not been
resented. Time and again he said "This was not cruel—this was kind
treatment." Dr. Blacker said this method of training had produced
great self-control and depth of wisdom-compassion, and we were not
likely to meet another like him.

As a final contribution Mr. Humphreys then read a collated series
of extracts from the Memorial Volume of *The Eastern Buddhist,* each
bringing out some quality in Dr. Suzuki which the writer wished to
emphasize. He closed with a memorable extract from the contribution of Father Thomas Merton.

Speaking for myself, I can venture to say that in Dr. Suzuki, Buddhism
finally became for me completely comprehensible, whereas before it had been
a very mysterious and confusing jumble of words, images, doctrines, legends,
rituals, buildings, and so forth. It seemed to me that the great and baffling
cultural luxuriance which has clothed the various forms of Buddhism in

different parts of Asia is the beautiful garment thrown over something quite simple. The greatest religions are all, in fact, very simple. They all retain very important essential differences, no doubt, but in their inner reality they all end up with the simplest and most baffling thing of all: direct confrontation with Absolute Being, Absolute Love, Absolute Mercy or Absolute Void, by an immediate and fully awakened engagement in the living of everyday life. In Christianity the confrontation is theological and affective, through word and love. In Zen it is metaphysical and intellectual through insight and emptiness. Yet Christianity too has its tradition of apophatic contemplation or knowledge in "unknowing," while the last words I remember Dr. Suzuki saying (before the usual good-byes) was "*The most important thing is Love!*" I must say that as a Christian I was profoundly moved. Truly *Prajñā* and *Karuṇā* are one.

Closing the meeting Mr. Humphreys said: "May I close with an apt quotation from Chuang-Tzu, whom Dr. Suzuki regarded as the greatest philosopher of China. 'The master came because it was his time to be born; he went because it was his time to die. For those who accept the phenomenon of birth and death in this sense, lamentation and sorrow have no place.' Nevertheless, we shall remember, bearing in mind this sound advice, 'Seek not to follow in the footsteps of the Ancient Ones. Seek what they sought.' Peace be with him."

The audience sat for a while until the deep notes of the bronze gong had slowly died away.

# The Development of Mahāyāna Buddhism

This article was written for the Buddhist Review, the journal of the newly formed Buddhist Society in Great Britain and Ireland, in 1909. Concerning the use of the term Hīnayāna, meaning smaller vehicle (of liberation) as distinct from the Mahāyāna, large vehicle, Dr. Suzuki refers to the "historical odium" of the former term but retains it for convenience. I have done the same throughout and the article appears as first published.—ED.

European Buddhist scholars are accustomed to divide Buddhism into two, Northern and Southern. They understand by Southern Buddhism that which mostly prevails in Ceylon, Burma, and Siam, while Northern Buddhism is represented by Tibetan Lamaism, as well as by that in China, Korea, and Japan. This geographical division, however, does not seem to be quite correct or justifiable, for we know that the Buddhism of Tibet is as different from the Buddhism of Japan, as it is from that of Ceylon or Burma, not only in some of its teachings but principally in its practical aspect. Take, for instance, the Chinese or Japanese Zen Sect (Ch'an in Chinese and Dhyāna in Sanskrit), or the Sect of the Pure Land, and compare it with Tibetan Buddhism as it is known today, and it will be found that the difference between the two is wider perhaps than that between the so-called Southern Buddhism, and one of the Japanese or Chinese Buddhist sects, known as Risshu (Li in Chinese and Vinaya in Sanskrit).

It is probably better to divide Buddhism into the Buddhism of Arhats and that of Bodhisattvas, understanding by the former, that Buddhism whose ideal attainment is Arhatship, and by the Buddhism of Bodhisattvas, that system of Buddhist teaching, which makes the conception of Bodhisattvahood its most prominent feature. Or we can retain the old way of classifying the followers of Buddhism into the

1

Mahāsāṅghika and the Sthavira, or even invent a new method of division, and call the one progressionists and the other conservatives.

Taking all in all, however, it seems that the distinction of Mahāyāna and Hīnayāna Buddhism is preferable to all the rest, as far as our present knowledge of the development of Buddhism is concerned. Of course, this distinction recalls an historical odium, which it is best for modern scholars to avoid. Neglecting this latter objection, the term Mahāyāna is comprehensive and definite enough to include all those schools of Buddhism, in which the ideal of Bodhisattvahood is upheld in preference to the attainment of Arhatship, and whose geographical distribution covers not only the Northern parts of India but extends eastward. Let us therefore use the term Mahāyāna in this article more for the sake of practical convenience than anything else, until the time arrives when Buddhism is thoroughly studied in all its diverse aspects, historical, dogmatic, ritualistic, etc.

The object of the present article is to expound briefly, what in our opinion constitutes the essential characteristics of the Mahāyāna Buddhism, in contradistinction to the Hīnayāna Buddhism.

If one wishes to sum up Mahāyānism in one word, it can be said that it is essentially speculative. Buddhism generally teaches three forms of discipline: moral, contemplative, and intellectual; and of these the last seems to have been particularly emphasized by the Mahāyānists, while moral discipline has become the chief feature of Southern Buddhism, so called—in fact, to such an extent, that most Western students of Buddhism, whose principal source of information is the Pāli Tipitaka, are apt to take Buddhism as neither more nor less than a sort of ethical culture society, which therefore must not be called a religious system in the same sense of Christianity. While the Buddha apparently taught a well-balanced practice of *Śīla, Dhyāna,* and *Prajñā,* his followers became one-sided, as is generally the case with all religious teachings, and emphasized one point at the expense of others. Mahāyānism in one sense can be said to have gone too far in its speculative flight, almost to the point of forgetting its ethical code, the *Vinaya,* while the Hīnayāna adherents are apt to bring upon themselves the criticism of too much conservatism, and a refusal to adapt themselves to their ever-changing environment. Whether these criticisms be well-founded or not, a practical reformer of Buddhism today, would do well to endeavour to restore the equilibrium between the three forms of discipline, and thus carry out more perfectly the original spirit of its founder.

This one-sided development of the two forms of Buddhism can also be seen in their respective histories. In Ceylon, there has been practically but one sect ever since its introduction. The Singhalese Buddhists have one code of morality, the *Vinaya,* which is recorded in detail in their scriptures, and which, being so explicit in its enunciation that even the unlearned could comprehend it readily, does not allow any very widely divergent interpretations. Accordingly, there were few chances of dissent. The *Vinaya* as it is practiced today in Ceylon has not changed perhaps, even in its details, since the day of its first promulgation in that island. In this respect, we can say that Hīnayāna Buddhism faithfully preserves the practical form of Buddhist moral culture as it developed during the time that elapsed between the decease of the Buddha and the despatch of the Aśoka missionaries to Ceylon. We emphasize this latter point, for it is quite reasonable to suppose, as is justified by the records in our possession, that Buddhism began to change, among the Buddha's variously-endowed disciples, soon after his time.

History, however, records quite a different state of affairs among the Mahāyānists. Into how many schools did it divide itself, and how vehemently did each school contend for its own doctrines against the others? While the Hīnayānists evidently kept quiet, the Mahāyānists treated their fellow-believers in a way which was not in perfect accord with their professed liberalism. In fact, it was through their self-conceit, that they came to designate themselves as Mahāyāna Buddhists, followers of the Great Vehicle of Salvation, to the disparagement of their somewhat conservative brothers in the faith. This spirit of self-exaltation was exhibited, not only against those in a sense the more orthodox ethical adherents of Buddhism, but also among themselves, as is seen in the policy of the famous founder of the Nichiren or Puṇḍarīka Sect in Japan. His denunciation of the other Buddhist sects then existing in his country was so strong and vehement and almost abusive that the authorities of the time thought it expedient quietly to get rid of him, though we must add that his prosecution was not entirely for religious reasons.

This struggle and conflict, however, was in accord with the somewhat one-sided development of Mahāyānism in the direction of speculative philosophy. Intellect is always inclined to dissent, to quarrel, to become self-conceited, and the rise of the ten or twelve sects of Japanese Buddhism was the inevitable result of the Mahāyāna movement in general. Of course, they have not forgotten phases of Buddhism other than intellectual, for the practice of *dhyāna* is still in evidence—indeed, there is one sect in Japan and China bearing the very name, and exercising much influence especially among the educated classes, but the fact remains that the Mahāyāna Buddhism is a development of one side—the intellectual, speculative, philosophical side—of Buddhism, while Hīnayānism preserves its ethical ideals. To realize the perfect form of Buddhism, the threefold treasure, triratna, must be equally developed: the Buddha, the Dharma, and the Sangha must stand side by side, imbued with the same spirit as when they were first established, whatever outward transformation they may have undergone. If Hīnayānism is said to preserve the Sangha in its perfect form, Mahāyānism may be considered to have fully developed the religio-philosophical significance of Buddhism, while both schools claim the Buddha as their common founder. The problem that faces faithful Buddhists at present is how best to effect a complete reconciliation of the moral discipline of Hīnayānism with the speculations of Mahāyānism.

Now in order to see how Mahāyānism has developed speculation as compared with Hīnayānism, we will first discuss the doctrine of *Anātman,* or "non-ego." This is considered to be one of the most important and characteristic features of Buddhism, and justly so, for both the Hīnayāna and the Mahāyāna uphold this as essential. The Hīnayāna school, however, seems to have remained almost too faithful, as it were, to the doctrine—it has not gone beyond its negative statement, it has not carried out its logical consequence to its utmost limits; while Mahāyānism has not only extended the theory from its subjective significance to the objective world, but has also boldly developed the positive conclusion implied in it. We do not mean that the Hīnayāna has none of the tendencies shown by the Mahāyāna; in fact, the former seems to contain everything Mahāyānistic in its germinal form, if we may use the term. What most conspicuously distinguishes the Mahāyāna school in this connection is that it makes most explicit, manifest, unequivocal, and fearless assertions on the religio-philosophical questions which deeply concern the human heart.

In the case of the non-ego theory, the Mahāyānists assert that there is no *ātman* or ego-soul not only in its subjective aspect but in its objective application. That is to say, they deny with the Hīnayāna followers

that there is such a thing as the ego-substance behind our consciousness, as a concrete, simple, ultimate, and independent unit; but they go
still further and declare that this objective world too has no *ātman*, no
ego, no God, no personal creator, no *Īśvara*, working and enjoying his
absolute transcendence behind this eternal concatenation of cause and
effect. This is technically known as the double negation of the subjective and the objective world, and for this reason the Mahāyāna
school has often been called, though unjustifiably and quite incorrectly,
nihilism or *śūnyavādin*.

It may be interesting to quote a Western Buddhist scholar's opinion
of Buddhism as typical of a prejudiced and uncritical judge. Eitel, a
noted student of Chinese Buddhism, thus speaks of the Buddhist
doctrine of Nirvāṇa in his "Three Lectures on Buddhism," delivered in
Union Church, Hong Kong, 1870–1871. "Nirvāṇa is to them (Buddhists) a state of which nothing can be said, to which no attributes can
be given; it is altogether an abstract, devoid alike of all positive and all
negative qualities. What shall we say of such empty, useless speculations, such sickly, dead words, whose fruitless sophistry offers to that
natural yearning of the human heart after an eternal rest, nothing better
than a philosophical myth? It is but natural that a religion which started
with moral and intellectual bankruptcy should end in moral and intellectual suicide." (Page 21, col. 2)

As a matter of fact, the Mahāyānists do not regard negation as the
ultimate goal of their speculations; for with them negation is but a road
to reach a higher form of affirmation, and they are aware of the fact
that the human mind lives in affirmation, and not in negation. Any
critic of Mahāyāna philosophy, who has sufficient sympathetic insight
to penetrate deep enough into its heart, would readily find that behind
the series of negations offered by the Mahāyāna thinkers there is really
the assertion of a higher truth, which, owing to the limitations of the
human mind, cannot be represented by any other means than negation.
It is not on account of sophistry or mere abstraction, that Buddhists
sometimes appear to delight in a negative state of truth. They are most
earnestly religious, they know that the deepest religious truth cannot be
presented in a stereotyped philosophical formula. Only those who are
timidly shortsighted, stop at the negation and refuse to go beyond, and
if they thus misjudge the signification of Mahāyāna Buddhism, the
fault is on their own side.

What is then that positive something offered by Mahāyāna scholars as the logical conclusion of the theory of non-ego? It is generally designated as *Tattva* or Suchness. This is a philosophical term, and when its religious import is emphasized, it is called *Dharmakāya*. The term, *Dharmakāya,* is very difficult to define. Essence-Body, Being-Body, Being-System does not exactly express all the ideas contained in it. Dharma is a very comprehensive term in Buddhist philosophy, and in this case it means essence, being, law, and doctrine. In short let us understand *Dharmakāya* here as the source, the ultimate reality, from which is derived the reason of existence, morality, and religion. In this conception of Suchness, or *Dharmakāya,* Mahāyānists find the highest possible affirmation reached after a series of negations, and unifying all forms of contradiction, psychological, ethical, and ontological. Aśvaghoṣa, one of the greatest of the early Indian Buddhist philosophers, says in his *Awakening of Faith in the Mahāyāna,*[1] "Suchness is neither that which is existent, nor that which is non-existent; it is neither that which is at once existent and non-existent, nor that which is not at once existent and non-existent; it is neither that which is one, nor that which is many; neither that which is at once one and many, nor that which is not at once one and many. . . . It is altogether beyond the conception of the human intellect, and the best way of designating it seems to be to call it Suchness."

Nāgārjuna, the founder of the Mādhyamika school of Buddhism in India, who was equally great as Aśvaghoṣa, declares in his *Treatise on the Mean,* "No birth, no death, no persistence, no oneness, no many-ness, no coming, no departing: . . . this is the doctrine of the Mean." Again, "To think, 'it is,' is eternalism: to think 'it is not,' is nihilism. To be and not to be, the wise cling to neither."

All these statements have been construed as nihilistic and leading the mind nowhere but to absolute emptiness. But, as we have said before, such critics entirely ignore the fact that the human understanding, owing to its constitutional shortcomings, often finds it most expedient and indeed most logical to state a truth in the form of a negation, as really expressing a higher form of affirmation, and comprehended only through a process of intuition. The Mahāyāna thinkers have denied with their conservative fellow-believers the existence of a concrete ego-soul;

[1]Translated by the author from the Chinese, 1900.

they have refused to accept the doctrine of a personal God; they are further reluctant to assert anything dogmatically; and the ultimate logical consequence of all these necessarily negative statements could not be anything else than the conception of Suchness. Beyond this, one enters upon mysticism—philosophy must bow her head modestly at this gate of Suchness, and let religion proceed by herself into an unknown wilderness, or "Wülde, or "Abgrund," as the German mystics are fond of designating this realm of "Eternal Yes," or that which is the same thing, of "Eternal No." At this point, therefore, Mahāyānism becomes mysticism. Intellectually, it has gone as far as it could. *Vidyā* must give way to *dhyāna* or *Prajñā,* that is, intellect to intuition, which is after all the ultimate goal of all religious discipline. Mysticism is the life of religion; without it religion loses the reason of its existence—all its warm vitality is gone, all its inexpressible charms vanish, and there remains nothing but the crumbling bones and the cold ashes of death. We said before that Mahāyānism was highly speculative, but it must now be added that it is most deeply and thoroughly religious.

It is apparent that with the conception of Suchness, Mahāyāna speculations have reached their culminating point, and upon this stands the grand religious edifice of Mahāyāna Buddhism. Superficially, Mahāyānism seems very different from Hīnayānism; but when its development is traced along the lines indicated above, one will readily comprehend that in spite of the disparity which exists between the two yānas of Buddhism, the one is no more than a continuity of the other, which started intellectually and ends in speculative mysticism.

When the conception of Suchness is established, the reason of Mahāyānism becomes evident. Buddhism is no more an agnostic system than a system of atheistic ethics. For in Suchness or *Dharmakāya* it finds the reason of existence, the true reality, the norm of morality, the source of love and goodness, the fountain head of righteousness, absolute intelligence, and the starting point of karma—for Suchness, according to the Mahāyāna thinkers, is not a mere state of being, but it is energy, intelligence, and love. But as Suchness begins to take these attributes upon itself, it ceases to be transcendental Suchness; it is now conditioned Suchness. So long as it remained absolutely transcendental, allowing neither negation nor affirmation, it was beyond the ken of the human understanding, and could not very well become the object of our religious consciousness. But there was the awakening of a will in

Suchness, and with this awakening we have conditional and self-limiting Suchness in place of the absolutely unknowable. (As to the why and how of this process, we have to confess a profound and eternal ignorance.) It is in this transformation, so to speak, of Suchness that the Mahāyāna system recognizes the religious significance of *Dharmakāya*.

The *Dharmakāya* is now conceived by the human heart as love and wisdom, and its eternal prayer is heard to be the deliverance of the ignorant from their self-created evil karma which haunts them as an eternal curse. The process of deliverance is to awaken in the mind of the ignorant the *Samyaksambodhi*, or most perfect wisdom, which is the reflection of the *Dharmakāya* in sentient beings. This wisdom, this *Bodhi*, is generally found asleep in the benighted, who are in a spiritual slumber induced by the narcotic influence of evil karma, which has been and is being committed by them, because of their non-realization of the presence in themselves of the *Dharmakāya*. Deliverance or enlightenment, therefore, consists of making every sentient being open his mental eye to this fact. It is not his ego-soul that makes him think, feel, desire, or aspire, but the *Dharmakāya* itself in the form of *Bodhicitta* or "wisdom-heart" which constitutes his ethical and religious being. Abandon the thought of egoism, and return to the universal source of love and wisdom, and we are released from the bond of evil karma, we are enlightened as to the reason of existence, we are Buddhas.

In trying to make a sentient being realize the presence in himself of the *Bodhicitta*, the *Dharmakāya* can be said to be working for its own awakening. Here is involved a great philosophical and religious problem. In the beginning, the *Dharmakāya* negated itself by its own affirmation, and it is now working to release itself from the negation, through which this world of particulars was created. This is, as it seems to our limited intellect, an eternal process of Suchness, from affirmation to negation, and from negation to affirmation. To this mystery of mysteries, however, we fail to apply our rules of syllogism, we have simply to state the truth, apparently contradictory, that our religious consciousness finds in this mystery something unspeakably fascinating and indeed the justification of her own eternal yearning.

At any rate, as a consequence of the conception of Suchness or *Dharmakāya* as eternal motherhood, as the source of infinite love, the doctrine of karma had to modify, as it were, its irrefragable severity. Here we observe another phase of differentiation as effected by the Mahāyānists from the doctrine commonly held by their ethical, monastic brethren; we do not maintain that the doctrine of karma is denied by Mahāyāna thinkers, far from it. They adhere to the doctrine as firmly as the Hīnayāna philosophers; they have taken away only its crushing effects upon the sinful, who are always too timid, too weak-hearted to bear the curse of all their former evil deeds. In other words, the Mahāyāna Buddhists offer a doctrine complementary to that of karma, in order to give a more satisfying and more human solution to our inmost religious needs. The Mahāyāna doctrine of *Pariṇāmanā*, therefore, must go side by side with that of karma; for through this harmonious co-working of the two, the true spirit of Buddhism will be more effectively realized. In this phase of development, Mahāyāna Buddhism must be said to be profoundly religious.

The doctrine of *Pariṇāmanā* is essentially that of vicarious sacrifice. Apparently it contradicts the continuity of karmaic activity; but in Mahāyāna Buddhism, it must be remembered, karma is conceived more in its cosmic aspect than individualistically, and it is therefore possible to reconcile the two notions, karma and *Pariṇāmanā*. We will try to make this point clear.

First, what does *Pariṇāmanā* mean? It comes from the root *nam*, to which is prefixed the particle *pari*, and we take the term as meaning "to bend toward," "to deliver," "to transfer," or "to renounce," for which the Chinese Buddhists use *hui shang*, meaning "to turn in the direction of." The doctrine of *Pariṇāmanā*, then, is to turn one's merit over to another, to renounce oneself for another, to sacrifice one's interests for the benefit of others, to atone for the evil karma of others by one's own good deeds, or to substitute oneself for another, who ought properly speaking to suffer his own karma. To use Christian terminology, the doctrine of *Pariṇāmanā* is in some respects identical with the doctrine of vicarious sacrifice; but it must be remembered that while vicarious sacrifice in Christianity means the death of Christ on the cross for the sin of mankind, the Mahāyānists do not confine the principle to a solitary historical incident. Christianity is built upon the history of a person, whatever its intrinsic authenticity, and not directly upon intellectual necessity and the facts of religious consciousness. Therefore, it is unable to uphold the universal application of the principal of vicarious sacrifice, and cannot appreciate the importance of the principle of karma. Herein lies the strength of Christianity, the strength of concreteness and objectivity, as compared with Mahāyāna Buddhism; but herein lies also its weakness—at least so it seems to Buddhist thinkers. A religion built upon history naturally appeals more vividly to our imagination, but the foundation does not seem so firm, as that of one which derives its sanction directly from the human heart.

The Mahāyāna notion of *Pariṇāmanā* is based upon the following truths: The universe is a grand spiritual system composed of moral beings, who are so many fragmentary reflexes of the *Dharmakāya*. The system is so closely knitted together that when any part of it or any unit composing it is affected in any way, good or bad, all the other parts or units are drawn into the general commotion which follows, and share the common fate. This subtle spiritual system, of which all sentient beings are its parts or units, is like a vast ocean in which the eternal moonlight of *Dharmakāya* is reflected. Even a faint wavelet which is noticed in one part of the water is sure to spread, sooner or later, according to the resistance of the molecules, over its entire surface, and thus finally disturb the serenity of the lunar image in it. Likewise, at every deed, good or evil, committed by any of the sentient units of this spiritual organization, the *Dharmakāya* rejoices or is grieved. When it is grieved, it wills to counteract the evil with goodness; when it rejoices, it knows that so far the cause of goodness has been advanced. Individual karma, therefore, is not really individual, it is most intimately connected with the whole, and is not an isolated phenomenon originating from the individual and returning to the same agent. In fact, it is no mere abstraction to say that the lifting of my arm or the moving of my leg is not an accidental, indifferent act, but is directly related to the ultimate cause of the universe. This assertion applies with an immeasurably greater emphasis to an act which has a moral bearing. "If," we can ask ourselves, "in our spiritual plan of existence things are so intimately related to one another, why could we not make the merit of our own deeds compensate or destroy the effect of an evil karma created by an ignorant mind? Why could we not suffer for the sake of others, and lighten, even to a small degree, the burden of evil karma under which weak and ignorant ones are groaning, though they have nobody but themselves to blame for their own wretchedness?" These questions were answered by Mahāyāna thinkers, affirmatively. They said, "It is possible for us to dedicate our own good karma to the cause of universal goodness, and to suppress or crush or to make quite inefficacious the evil karma perpetrated by the ignorant. It is possible for us to substitute ourselves for others and to bear the burden in their behalf, thus saving them from their self-created curse." The result of this conviction is the doctrine of *Pariṇāmanā*.

In this, therefore, it is seen that quite in accordance with the cosmic conception of *Dharmakāya*, Mahāyāna philosophers emphasize the universal or supra-individual significance of karma more than its solitary, individual character. In the Hīnayāna system, the conception of karma is individualistic pure and simple, there is no escape whatever from the consequence of one's evil or good deeds, for it follows one even after death which is merely another form of birth. The Mahāyāna Buddhists believe in this as far as the law of karmaic causation is concerned, but they go one step further and assert that karma has also its cosmic or supra-individual aspect which must be taken into consideration when we want to realize fully the meaning of our spiritual existence. Though a man had to reap what he had sown, and there were no possible escape from the consequence of his evil deeds, the Mahāyānists would say, a Bodhisattva wishes from his fullness of heart to turn over to the general welfare of his community whatever merit he can have from his acts of goodness, and to bear upon himself whatever burden of evil is going to befall his ignorant, self-destroying fellow-beings. The good he does is not necessarily for his own interest; the evil he avoids is not always for his own benefit; whatever deed he performs, he does not forget its universal character; above all, he desires to be of service in any capacity to the whole spiritual community of which he is a unit.

In point of fact, therefore, the doctrine of *Pariṇāmanā* is more than that of vicarious sacrifice. It is that, in so far as a Bodhisattva wishes to bear the burden of evil for the real offenders, and to save them from sufferings, but when he works to add to the "general stock of goodness," and to nourish the "root of merit" in this world, he is doing more than merely substituting, he is doing something positive. *Pariṇāmanā* is vicarious sacrifice, self-renunciation, the transference of merit, the promotion of universal goodness, the annihilation of "me" and "thee," the recognition of the oneness of all things, and the complete satisfaction of our inmost religious yearnings.

The doctrine of karma is terrible; the doctrine of *Pariṇāmanā* is humane: karma is the law of nature, inflexible and irreconcilable; *Pariṇāmanā* is the heart of a religious being, filled with tears: the one is rigidly masculine and knows no mercy whatever; the other is most tenderly feminine, always ready to weep and help: the one is justice incarnate; the other is absolute love: the one is the god of thunder and lightning, who crushes everything that dares to resist him; the other is a gentle spring shower, warm, soft, and relaxing, and helping all life to grow: we bow before the one in awe and reverence; we embrace the other as if finding again the lost mother: we must have the one to be responsible for our own thoughts, feelings, aspirations, and deeds; but we cannot let the other go, as we need love, tolerance, humaneness, and kindheartedness. Mahāyāna Buddhism can thus be said to have a singularly softening effect on the conception of karma. Karma cannot be denied, it is the law; but the human heart is tender and loving, it cannot remain calm and unconcerned at the sight of suffering, in whatever way this might have been brought about. It knows that all things ultimately come from the one source; when others suffer I suffer too; why then should not self-renunciation somehow moderate the austerity of karma? This is the position taken by Mahāyāna Buddhists in regard to the doctrine of karma.

With the moderation, as it were, of karmaic theory, another change took place in the system of Mahāyāna Buddhism concerning the notion of an ideal man, that is, as to what constitutes the true ideal Buddhist, or what kind of being he must be, who really embodies all the noble thoughts and enlightened sentiments of Mahāyāna Buddhism. Arhatship was not quite satifactory in this respect, and ceased to be the goal of religious discipline for the followers of the Mahāyāna. They considered the Arhat as one not fully realizing all the inmost aspirations of the religious consciousness, for he was a Buddhist who sought only his own deliverance from the whirlpool of birth and death, in which all beings are struggling and being drowned. So long as karma was looked upon in its individualistic aspect, Arhatship was quite the right thing for the Buddhists to aspire after; but karma could be interpreted in another and wider sense, which made the doctrine of *Pariṇāmanā* possible, and Mahāyānists thought that this was more in accord with the deepest yearnings of a religious being, who wants to save not only himself but the entire world as well. Therefore, the speculative Buddhists came to establish the ideal of Bodhisattvahood in place of Arhatship; and for this reason Mahāyānism is often designated as Bodhisattvayāna, in contradistinction to Śrāvakayāna and Pratyekabuddhayāna.

The development of the ideal of Bodhisattvahood was quite natural with Mahāyāna Buddhists. Grant that the followers of the Hīnayāna more faithfully adhered to the moral, monastic, and disciplinary life of primitive Buddhism, while the Mahāyānists were bent on the unfolding of the religio-philosophical significance of the teachings of Buddha, and it will be seen that the further they go, the wider is their separation from each other. To the moralists, such a bold flight of imagination, as that conceived by the Mahāyānists, was a very difficult thing to realize; moral responsibility implies a strict observance of the law of karma; what one has done cannot be undone; good or bad, one has to suffer the karmaic consequence. Nobody can interfere with it; Arhatship alone, therefore, could be made the goal of those self-disciplining moralists. With the Mahāyānists, however, it was different. They came to look at the import of our moral action more from the point of view of its cosmic relations, or from that of the most intimate interdependence that obtains among all sentient beings, in their moral, intellectual, and spiritual activities. With this change of point of view, they could not but come to the realization of the doctrine of *Pariṇāmanā.*

There are not two Buddhisms; the Mahāyāna and the Hīnayāna are one, and the spirit of the founder of Buddhism prevails on both. Each has developed in its own way, according to the difference of environment in which each has thrived and grown—understanding by environment all those various factors of life that make up the peculiarities of an individual or a nation. The lack of communication has hitherto prevented the bringing together of Buddhists, and they have therefore not yet arrived at a complete understanding of one another. The time is ripening now when each will fully realize and candidly admit its own shortcomings and advantages, and earnestly desire to cooperate with others to bring about a perfect assimilation of all Buddhist thoughts and practices into one uniform system, and thus contribute to the promotion of peace and goodwill towards all beings, regardless of their racial and national differences.

# The Message of Bodhidharma
## FOUNDER OF ZEN BUDDHISM

The history of Zen Buddhism starts with Bodhidharma, popularly known as Daruma in Japan and Tama in China, who came to China late in the fifth century. But the significance of Daruma was not fully recognized until the time of Yeno (Hui-neng in Chinese) when a dispute arose between him and his opponent, Junshu (Shen hsiu). They were both disciples of Gunin (Hung-ien, died 675) and each claimed to transmit the orthodox line of the Zen teaching traceable to the First Patriarch, Bodhidharma. This being the case, we can say that the value and signification of Zen Buddhism as distinct from all the other schools of Buddhism so far developed in China was not manifestly appreciated by its followers until late in the seventh century.

What is then the teaching of Daruma? Three characteristic features of it may be pointed out as distinguishable from other Buddhist schools. As Daruma's teaching, which later came to be known as Zen Buddhism, belongs to the practical wing of the Mahāyāna it does not attempt to offer any novel method of philosophizing on the truth of Buddhism. Daruma was no logician. He simply wanted to live the truth. Whatever he taught, therefore, consisted in presenting a method considered by him to be most effective in the attainment of the final goal of the Buddhist life. The characteristic features of his teaching are thus inevitably all related to the Buddhist discipline.

(1) The first thing needed for the discipline then was to know definitely what the objective of the Buddhist life was. Without full knowledge of this, the yogin would be like a blind man running wild. Daruma pointed out that the objective was to see into the nature of one's own being, and this he designated *shin* or *kokoro* (or *hsin* in Chinese). *Shin* or *hsin* corresponds to the Sanskrit *citta* but fre-

14

quently to *hridaya.* When it is translated as "mind," it is too intellectual; "heart" is too emotional; while "soul" suggests something concrete—it is so strongly associated with an ego-substance. Provisionally I shall make Mind with a capital "M" perform the office of *shin* or *hsin.* Now Daruma wants us to see into this Mind. For it is only when this is perceived or grasped that we attain the end which is the "peaceful settling of the mind" called *anjin (an-hsin).*

Daruma's interview with Eka (Hui-k'e) is significant in this respect. He did not talk about realizing Nirvāṇa, or attaining emancipation; nor did he discourse on the doctrine of non-ego, that is *anatta.* When Eka told his master how troubled he was in his mind, the latter at once demanded that he produce this troubled mind before him so that he could calm it for its owner. For this was Daruma's patented method, which had not yet been resorted to by any of his predecessors.

When Eka complained about his mind being in trouble, he used the term "mind" in its conventional meaning, which, however, indicated also that his thought followed the conventional line of reasoning. That is to say, he cherished an unconscious belief in the reality of an entity known as mind or *shin,* and this belief further involved a dualistic interpretation of existence leading to the conceptual reconstruction of experience. As long as such a belief was entertained, one could never realize the end of the Buddhist discipline. Daruma, therefore, wished to liberate Eka from the bondage of the idea of a mind. Liberation was a "pacific settlement" of it, which was at the same time the seeing into the inner nature of one's own being, the Mind.

Eka must have spent many years in this search for a mind, with which he was supposed to be endowed, philosophically or logically as well as conventionally. Finally, it must have dawned upon him that there was after all no such entity as to be known as mind. But this recognition failed to ease his mind, because it still lacked a final "stamping"; it did not break out in his consciousness as a final experience. He appeared again before Daruma and gave an answer to the master's former demand for a mind: "I seek for the mind but it is not attainable." Daruma now exclaimed, "I have your mind peacefully settled!"

Eka now had a real experience; this authoritative "stamping" on the part of the master broke the intellectual barrier and made Eka go beyond the mere formulation of his insight as the unattainability of a mind. Without Daruma's absolute confirmation, Eka did not know yet where to have his "mind" fixed. A fixing was no-fixing, and therefore the fixing, to use the *Prajñā* dialectic. In other words, Eka found his "mind" where it was not to be found, and thus his "mind" came to be finally peacefully settled. This is Daruma's doctrine of Mind.

(2) Did Daruma teach us any definite form of meditation? Zen means *dhyāna,* i.e. meditation. Being the First Patriarch of Zen in China, Daruma naturally advocates meditation. But his is the one specifically known as *Hekkwan (pi-kuan),* literally "wall-gazing." He has never defined the term and it is difficult to know exactly what kind of meditation it was. This much we can say, that as long as it was differentiated from the traditional method and claimed to be Mahāyānistic, it was not mere tranquilization, nor was it a form of contemplation. It was to follow the idea referred to in the *Vimalakīrti:* "When a mind is controlled so as to be steadily fixed on one subject, such a one will accomplish anything." This means "to keep mind as self-concentrated as a rigidly standing cliff, with nothing harassing its imperturbability." For thereby one can enter the Path *(tao).*

Daruma's *Hekkwan,* therefore, means "concentration," fixing attention steadily on one subject. But there must have been something more in it. The *Hekkwan* was the method of finding out the "abode of all thoughts," in other words, of having an insight into the nature of Mind. The method is always defined and controlled by the object. When the object is to experience what is immovable in the movable without stopping its movement, the self-concentration means a state of utmost activity, and not at all mere quietude or passivity. The *Hekkwan* then in connection with its object begins to have a definite signification of its own.

In fact "wall-gazing" is not at all appropriate to explain the *Hekkwan.* "To stand rigidly like a cliff" does not mean the bodily posture assumed by the Zen practicer when he sits cross-legged with his backbone straight. "Being like a cliff or wall" refers to an inner state of mind in which all disturbing and entangling chains of ideas are cut asunder. The mind has no hankerings now; there is in it no looking around, no reaching out, no turning aside, no picturing of anything; it is like a solid rock or a block of wood; there is neither life nor death in it, neither memory nor intellection. Although a mind is spoken of according to the conventional parlance, here there is really no "mind," the mind is no-mind, *shin* is *mushin, hsin* is *wu-hsin, citta* is *acitta*. This is the *Hekkwan* meditation.

But if we imagine this to be the final state of the exercise, we are greatly in the wrong, for we have not yet entered into the Path *(tao)*. The necessary orientation has been achieved, but the thing itself is far beyond. When we stop here, Zen loses its life. There must be a turning here, a waking-up, a new sense of awareness reached, the breaking of the deadlock, so to speak. All the intellectual attempts hitherto made to seek out the abode of all thoughts and desires could not come to this; all forms of contemplation, all the exercises of tranquilization hitherto advocated by the Indian and the Chinese predecessors of Daruma could not achieve this. Why? Because the objects they erected severally for their discipline were altogether amiss and had no inherent power of creation in them.

(3) What may be called the ethical teaching of Daruma's Zen Buddhism is the doctrine of *Mukudoku* (*wu-kung-te* in Chinese) which means "no merit." This is the answer given by Daruma to his Imperial inquirer as to the amount of merit to be accumulated by building temples, making offerings to the Buddha, providing shelters for monks and nuns, etc. According to the First Patriarch, deeds performed with any idea of merit accruing from them have no moral value whatever. Unless you act in accord with the "Dharma," which is by nature pure, beyond good and bad, you cannot be said to be a Zen follower.

According to Daruma, there is no antithesis in the Dharma of good and evil, of detachment and attachment, of "self" and "other." In Daruma's discourse on "the Twofold Entrance" he describes the life of a wise man in the following terms:

As there is in the essence of the Dharma no desire to possess, a wise man is ever ready to practice charity with his body, life and property, and he never begrudges—he never knows what an ill grace means. As he has a perfect understanding of the threefold nature of Emptiness *(śūnyatā)*, he is above partiality and attachment. Only because of his will to cleanse all beings of their stains, he comes among them as one of them, but he is not attached to form. This is the self-benefiting phase of his life. He, however, knows also how to benefit others and again how to glorify the truth of Enlightenment. As with the virtue of Charity, so with the other five virtues: Morality, Humility, Indefatigability, Meditation, and Intuition. That a wise man practices the six virtues of perfection is to get rid of confused thoughts, and yet there is no consciousness on his part that he is engaged in any meritorious deeds—which means to be in accord with the Dharma.

This concept of meritless deeds is one of the most difficult to understand—much more to practice. When this is thoroughly mastered the Zen discipline is said to have been mastered. The first intellectual approach to it is to realize that things of this world are characterized by polarity as they are always to be interpreted in reference to a subject which perceives and values them. We can never escape this polar opposition between subject and object. There is no absolute objective world from which a subject is excluded, nor is there any self-existing subject that has no objective world in any sense standing against it. But unless we escape this fundamental dualism we can never be at ease with ourselves. For dualism means finitude and limitation. This state of things is described by Mahāyānists as "attainable." An attainable mind is a finite one, and all worries, fears, and tribulations we go through are the machination of a finite mind. When this is transcended we plunge into the Unattainable, and thereby peace of mind is gained. The Unattainable is Mind.

This approach, being intellectual, is no more than a conceptual reconstruction of reality. To make it a living fact with blood and nerves, the Unattainable must become attainable, that is, must be experienced, for *anjin* (that is, peaceful settling of the mind) will then for the first time become possible.

In a recently recovered Tung-huang manuscript, which for various reasons I take to be discourses given by Daruma, the author is strongly against mere understanding according to words. The Dharma, according to him, is not a topic for discourse; the Dharma whose other name is Mind is not a subject of memory, nor of knowledge. When pressed for a positive statement, Daruma gave no reply, remaining silent. Is this not also a kind of meritless deed?

According to a Buddhist historian of the T'ang dynasty (618–907 A.D.) the coming of Daruma in China caused a great stir among the Buddhist scholars as well as among ordinary Buddhists, because of his most emphatically antagonistic attitude towards the latter. The scholars prior to him encouraged the study of Buddhist literature in the forms of *sūtras* and *śāstras;* and as the result there was a great deal of philosophical systematization of the dogmas and creeds. On the practical disciplinary side, the Buddhists were seriously engaged in meditation exercises, the main object of which was a kind of training in tranquilization. Daruma opposed this, too; for his *dhyāna* practice had the very high object of attaining to the nature of the Mind itself—and this not by means of learning and scholarship, nor by means of moral deeds, but by means of *Prajñā,* transcendental wisdom. To open up a new field in the Buddhist life was the mission of Daruma.

When Zen came to be firmly established after Yeno (Hui-neng) there grew among his followers a question regarding the coming of Daruma to China. The question was asked not for information, but for self-illumination. By this I mean that the question concerns one's own inner life, not necessarily anybody else's coming and going. While apparently Daruma is the subject, in reality he has nothing to do with it, and therefore in all the answers gathered below we notice no personal references whatever to Daruma himself.

In order to see what development characteristic of Zen Buddhism the teaching of Daruma made after the sixth patriarch, Yeno (Hui-neng), in China, I quote some of the responses made to the question cited above, in which the reader may recognize the working of the Mind variously given expression to:

UMMON YEN: Do you wish to know the Patriarch (Daruma)? So saying he took up his staff, and pointing at the congregation continued: The Patriarch is seen jumping over your heads. Do you wish to know where his eyes are? Look ahead and do not stumble?

KISU SEN: How did people fare before the coming of Daruma to China? Clean povery was fully enjoyed. How after his coming? Filthy wealth is the cause of many worries.

KEITOKU SEI: How were things before Daruma's coming to China? Six times six are thirty-six. How after his coming? Nine times nine are eighty-one.

GYOKU-SEN REN: How were things before Daruma's coming to China? Clouds envelop the mountain peaks. How after his coming? Rains fall on the Hsiao and the Hsiang.

HOUN HON: How as the world before Daruma's coming to China? The clouds dispersing, the three islets loom out clear. How after his coming? The rain passing, the flowers in hundreds are freshened up. What difference is there between before and after his coming? The boatman cleaving the light morning fog goes up the stream, while in the evening he comes down with the sail unfurled over the vapory waves.

To the question, "What is the meaning of Daruma's coming from the West?" the following answers are given by various masters:

RYUGE: This is the question hardest to crack.

RYOZAN KWAN: Don't make a random talk.

FUSUI GAN: Each time one thinks of it one's heart breaks.

SHOSHU: A happy event does not go out of the gate while a bad rumor travels a thousand miles.

DOSAN: I will tell you when the river Do begins to flow upward.

In Zen there is no uniform answer, as far as its apparent meaning is concerned, even to one and the same question, and the spirit is absolutely free in the choice of material when it wants to express itself.

# Zen Buddhism

"Zen" is an abbreviation of *Zazen,* which is Japanese; the Chinese original is *Ch'an* which is the translation of the Sanskrit term *Dhyāna;* in Pāli it is *Jhāna.* Chinese scholars do not like to use the original Sanskrit terms; they prefer every Sanskrit term to be translated into Chinese. When they find the Chinese equivalent of the original Sanskrit, then they try to blend the Chinese with the Sanskrit; a kind of hybrid is created in that way. To the Chinese mind these hybrid terms are very expressive and long usage has established words in that hybrid terminology as technical terms.

Now the terms *Ch'an* and *Za-zen* have been dropped and "Zen" alone is used. That means *Jhāna,* which, in its original sense, means "meditation"—not exactly mediation as used in the West, although something very similar to it. So *Jhāna* we may take to mean meditation, contemplation, tranquilization or concentration; such terms nearly express the original meaning of *Jhāna,* but not exactly. But the way in which Zen Buddhism uses the term "Zen" is quite different from its original meaning. This has to be emphasized at the outset.

Zen developed in China in the eighth century. It is traditionally ascribed to Bodhidharma, known as Tamo in China and Daruma in Japan. Bodhidharma came to China from India in the sixth century but what he taught was not exactly what came to be known as Zen. Zen really developed about 150 or 200 years after Bodhidharma came.

The real founder of Zen in China is known as Hui Neng, Wei Lang, or Yeno. What distinguished Hui Neng from his predecessors and from the rest of the Chinese Buddhist teachers is this, which really constitutes the essence of Zen teaching:

Enlightenment is an experience which Buddha had and through which he was able to teach Buddhism. Buddhism really means "the Doctrine of Enlightenment." *Prajñā* is used quite frequently as synonymous with enlightenment.

21

In China, previous to Yeno, it had been thought that this enlightenment could be attained only after one had practiced *Jhāna,* and attained proficiency in meditation. Yeno maintained that *Prajñā* and *Jhāna* should go together; neither alone would do. These two are considered most essential in the study of Buddhism.

There are three forms of discipline in the observance of Buddhism: (1) moral precepts, i.e., non-stealing, etc.; (2) *Jhāna* or Zen; and (3) *Prajñā.* Leaving aside the first, let us begin with Zen or *Jhāna* and *Prajñā.* Yeno said that *Jhāna* is *Prajñā* and *Prajñā* is *Jhāna.* Those two are not to be separated; one does not begin with *Jhāna* and then obtain *Prajñā.* Where there is *Prajñā* there is *Jhāna,* and *vice versa.* When one is attained the other comes with it; no separation between them is possible. This was his original teaching.

So when we say "Zen Buddhism," this "Zen" is used in a somewhat different sense from the ordinary one. Usually "Zen" is meditation, concentration or contemplation, but in Zen Buddhism "Zen" is used not in that sense but as synonymous with *Prajñā.* To understand Zen Buddhism, therefore, it is necessary to know that *Dhyāna* is not something different from *Prajñā* and that *Prajñā* is not something obtained after Zen is obtained. When we practice *Jhāna,* that is the very moment that *Prajñā* unfolds itself. This was the original teaching of Yeno and it was the beginning of Zen Buddhism.

One day a Chinese Government Officer who was also a poet and a painter called on the immediate disciple of Yeno and asked: "What is this one way; what is the teaching of your school which denies the distinction between "Zen" and "*Prajñā*"? The disciple of Yeno replied: "Zen is where you are talking; you ask a question and Zen is there. It is not that one comes before the other; they are simultaneous. When you talk to me there is Zen; there is *Prajñā*; they are not different."

To express this in a more modern way: while we are doing, thinking and feeling, there is this identity of Zen and *Prajñā.* This spatial intuitive knowledge is not to be developed after the practice of Zen. *Prajñā* is where Zen is.

*Prajñā* is another difficult term to translate into English. We generally use "transcendental wisdom" or "intuitive knowledge" to express *Prajñā.* The Chinese, in spite of their dislike for foreign languages, used a term which is the Chinese translation of *Prajñā. Prajñā* is something which our discursive knowledge cannot attain. It belongs to a different category from mere knowledge. Buddhists emphasize this distinction very much; they say, not knowing, but knowing and seeing; these two must come together. To know there must be two—subject and object.

Now, seeing is not just knowing about something; seeing is directly seeing it. Knowing and seeing are generally coupled in Buddhist teaching; knowing is not enough; seeing must come with knowing. In the West you distinguish between knowing and seeing. Knowing is philosophical, knowing about; and seeing is seeing directly, personally, i.e., by personal experience. Knowing always requires a mediator but seeing is direct, yet in seeing we do not generally see things directly. When we think we see something, that seeing is not real from the Zen point of view. When you see a flower, for example, not only must you see it but the flower must see you also; otherwise there is no real seeing. Seeing is really my seeing the flower and the flower seeing me. When this seeing is mutual there is real seeing.

Certain scholars say that when we think we see the flower, we put our feelings into the flower. My thinking or seeing or your thinking or seeing is put into the flower and the flower is given life. But, to the Zen way of thinking, there is no transference of my imagination into the flower. The flower itself is living and, as a living thing, sees me. So my seeing is also the flower seeing. When this takes place there is real seeing. When this end is achieved, i.e., when my seeing becomes the flower seeing, then there is real communication or real identification of the flower with myself, of subject with object. When this mutual identification takes place, the flower is myself and I am the flower.

A Chinese scholar once asked a Zen master, "One of the earlier Buddhist philosophers said, 'Heaven and earth are of the same source; ten thousand things and I are one.'" He added, "Is this not a wonderful saying?" The master looked at a flower in the courtyard and said, "Men of the world see this flower as in a dream," meaning that their seeing is not real seeing, which implies that for real seeing it is necessary for me to see the flower and for the flower to see me. When this is mutual and identification takes place, then there is real seeing. Then we experience what the Buddhist scholar stated in the passage just quoted: "Heaven and earth are of the same source; ten thousand things and I are one."

But this is mere abstract talk and so long as we are dealing with abstractions there is no actual experience. The Zen master pointed out this fact to his disciple: "Instead of talking about abstractions or quoting what others have said, do look at this flower which is now becoming and identify yourself with it, not as if you are in a dream, but see in actual reality the flower itself. Then you see that the whole universe is nothing but the expression of one's own mind."

Before I left Japan I read in an English journal an interesting article by a Russian whose idea was this: "The objective world can exist only in my subjectivity; the objective world does not really exist until it is experienced by this subjectivity or myself." That is something like Berkeley's Idealism. One day this Russian was riding his bicycle and he collided with a lorry; the driver was very angry but the Russian kept on saying, "The world is nothing but my subjectivity." On another occasion when he was thinking in the ordinary way, there was no collision but something else happened and he was awakened to this truth: "There is nothing but my subjectivity." When he experienced this, he had quite an illumination and he said to a friend. "Everything is in everything else." That means that all things are the same but he did not say that; he said, "Everything, each individual object, is in each other individual object. So this world of multitudes is not denied, as each thing is in every other one." This is most significant. When he expressed this to his friend, the friend could not understand but later he attained the same experience. This is *Prajñā*; this is transcendental wisdom, and when this intuition is attained, we have Zen. Zen is no other than this intuitive knowledge.

I must say more about this intuitive knowledge, or direct seeing. For example, if we touch fire the finger is burned; I feel intuitively that fire is dangerous without having to reason about it. When people talk about intuition it is connected with individual objects. There is someone who has an intuition and something in regard to which he has it. There is nothing between subject and object. These intuitions may take place immediately, i.e., without any intermediary; nevertheless there are subject and object, though their relationship is immediate instead of being through an intermediate agent. This kind of intuition we talk very much about but the intuition that Zen talks about is identification-seeing. That is, when I see the flower and the flower sees me, this kind of intuition or mutual identification is not individual seeing; it is not individual intuition. "I see the flower and the flower sees me" means that the flower ceases to be a flower. I cease to be myself. Instead there is unification. The flower vanishes into something higher than a flower and I vanish into that something higher than any individual object.

Now when this leveling up takes place, this being absorbed into
something higher than each relative being, it does not mean merely
being absorbed; there is intuition, awakening; there is something that
acknowledges itself to be itself, not annihilation or mere absorption
into the void. This "annihilation" is accompanied by intuition and that
is the most important point. When this takes place there is real seeing of
the flower. Therefore we can say that this—my seeing the flower and
the flower seeing me—takes place on a plane higher than that where the
flower is seen as an individual flower and I am seen as an individual
being. When there is absorption of the individual into something
higher, there is intuition. This is most important. This is in accordance
with the original teaching of Wei Lang. *Prajñā* is *Jhāna*.

Earlier teachers than Yeno had stated that when *Jhāna* was practiced
all things vanished and there was nothing left. By this it was meant that
no individual thing was left; but there is something which is not an
individual object; there is a perception of something and this perception
is intuition. This intuition is *Prajñā* or enlightenment and Yeno most
strongly emphasized this.

Now it may not be quite clear what Zen is driving at. I have a book
here which contains all the Zen sayings, starting with those of Bodhidharma. Bodhidharma may be a fictitious individual but that does not
matter; Yeno is historical. From him down to the early part of the Sung
Dynasty, about nine hundred years ago, this book contains all those
Chinese sayings called *Mondo*. The mind revolves, i.e., works, operates
as it faces ten thousand situations. When I see this lamp I see it
illuminated; when I touch this table, it is hard; so my mind moves
along; when I am struck, I feel. The mind moves in this way from one
sense to another just as things come along. This moving of the mind is
most subtle, obscure and mysterious.

When this table is struck I feel, but who is it that feels? What is it that
feels? When you try to get that person or mind or soul or spirit out here
and see it, you cannot. There is something you would like to get out of
yourself but you cannot; soul or spirit moves on all the time and this
moving on is subtle. When it is working in such a subtle way, when it is
going on, you can get hold of that something which cannot be taken
hold of. Then you have it. When you have that, then there is real
wisdom or *Prajñā*. When you have this *Prajñā*, then you are entirely
free from all sorrows, afflictions and all other things.

Now when I speak of being free from desires, tensions, fears, etc., you may think that the understanding of Zen will turn you into a piece of wood, insensitive, indifferent; but I do not say this. When I strike the table it feels pain as much as I would. You may say, "This is insane; it is not so." Everything is filled with sense, mind, heart. So when Buddha says to be free from desires and afflictions, this does not mean to become like a piece of wood; it means to make a piece of wood turn into a sensitive being. In a Chinese Zen monastery they have a heavy stick made of one piece of wood which they strike with a hammer and it is very sensitive. When a monk struck this, the master said, "I have a pain." That is not exaggerated; it really takes place. When they see a worm on the ground Buddhists try to avoid stepping on it. You may say that you cannot move an inch because something would be trodden on and die. True, you cannot move if you pursue this practice in its relative sense. But actually, when you have this intuitive understanding of things, you are like St. Francis of Assisi when he talked about "Our Brother Sun" and "Sister Moon" and befriended wolves and birds; he took everything as his own brother. His feeling was moving along the same lines, so there is no difference between the Christian and the Buddhist experience of final reality.

When Zen people talk about not having any feeling whatever, that does not mean no feeling on the relative plane, but no feeling based on selfish interests. To have no pain, no desires, does not mean to become cold ashes; it means to have no feeling in connection with selfish ideas. So long as we are individuals, we cannot but be selfish to some extent but this selfishness is not separate from that which is more than self. When self stays as self and does not expand to something higher than itself, that is the relative self. But when self finds itself enveloped, a component in something which is much wider and deeper, then it is not merely the relative self. When that kind of self is realized, enlightenment takes place. Zen Buddhism tries to make us attain that end.

Most Christians think that Christ was historically born at a certain place and time but, according to Eckhart, the great German philosopher of the thirteenth century, Christ is born in every one of us. When that is so, the relative self dies to itself and that relative self becomes empty. When the experience of uniformity, sameness and sensitivity takes place in our soul, it is then that Christ is born there. So every impediment or faulty particle of that which we call ourselves ought to be purged and the self ought to become really empty.

This is quite different from the ordinary Christian way of under-standing the birth of Christ but Eckhart had no knowledge whatever of Buddhism and Buddha had no knowledge of him, yet their teachings coincide perfectly. When I read Eckhart, I seem to be reading a Buddhist text with but a different terminology; so far as inner compre-hension is concerned, they are the same. This comprehension corre-sponds to intuition. Prehension is only grasping and touch is, I suppose, the most primitive sense, but this gives the purest feeling of identity; so prehension, taking hold of by the hand, is necessary. Sight is the most intellectual sense and hearing is next but there is a great distance between them and their object; whereas with touch there is an imme-diate coming together. We must experience that. It is the same as intuition, not just relative intuition but collective or total intuition. When this takes place there is real understanding of reality and the experience of Enlightenment. This is what constitutes the teaching of Zen as first taught by Yeno, Hui Neng or Wei Lang in the eighth century.

# The Spirit of Zen

The late Dr. D. T. Suzuki first visited the Society on July 20th 1936. Before arriving in England for the first Meeting of the World Congress of Faiths he sent us an article which appeared in the January–February issue of *Buddhism in England,* later *The Middle Way.* When he visited the Buddhist Lodge, as it was then called, on July 20th, at our house at 37 South Eaton Place, he found "a full house" with distinguished visitors including Dr. G. P. Malalasekera, Miss Constant Lounsbery, founder of Les Amis du Bouddhisme in Paris, Count Wachtmeister, who had composed a Buddhist opera, and Mr. T. K. Ch'u, who translated our version of the Tao Te Ching, the first to be translated into English by a Chinese.

After introducing Dr. Suzuki, I asked him "to help us to understand something of the spirit of Zen." The following article, from *Buddhism in England,* is a slightly edited transcript of a full note taken in short-hand by a member present.—ED.

Seeing that we are endowed with the power of speech and understand one another by means of this power, we have to appeal to words. But words are such an intractable medium. If we become masters of words we are all right, but sometimes we are too willingly slaves to words, and when words enslave us we become perfect fools. Zen Buddhism tries to master words, but the means it uses to help us in mastering them are strange, though not so strange to those who are used to them. But to others, they seem extraordinary.

How did Zen come to use such extraordinary methods in its teaching? When we ask that question we have to trace the history of the human intellect, and when we have traced it to its very source we will understand that the methods of Zen were something inevitable in the development of our spiritual life. As I cannot give the whole history of Zen, you must be satisfied with a very brief outline of how it developed in China and Japan. The Indian mind was rich in imagination and wonderful in its capacity for speculation. Indian metaphysics are the deepest in the world, and their dialects are incomparable. All nations of the world have to bow to the Indians in this respect. To them, religion was philosophy and philosophy religion, for whatever religion there is in India is backed by philosophy. Intellect should always be backed by certain deeper understandings which we may call faith. Intuition is the affirmation of a certain fundamental belief on which and with which and by which we stand and live our life. This must be associated with the intellect, and when it is associated it becomes a certain philosophy. That is the reason why, in India, religion is always associated with philosophy.

In Christianity theology is separate from Faith, but when Faith is left to itself it is apt to go astray. It becomes superficial and superstitious, leading in the end to bigotry. Faith represents the emotional side of human life, while philosophy is its intellectual side. Faith and philosophy must always go hand in hand, for when they are separated the result is lame. In India this philosophy was well in its way, but it lacked something which was supplied by the Chinese mind, something which we may call a consciousness of practical life, of life itself. In China morality became the foundation of society, and the Chinese people are prone to things practical. That is where the true greatness of the Chinese lies.

When Indian philosophy came to China as Buddhism, the Chinese people took to it partly, but at the same time there was something that did not quite appeal to them, something against which they revolted. "Zen," said a Chinese scholar, "is the revolt of the Chinese mind against Buddhism," It is a revolt. Yet while it is not quite Buddhism, it still is Buddhism. It developed from Buddhism, and in fact it could not have developed from anything else. Zen has its origin in India, but when it came to China this revolt of the Chinese mind gave it a somewhat different form.

The Zen form of Buddhism is deeply imbued with a practical spirit. For while there was logic and metaphysics in ancient China, it was never highly developed. They had a very subtle way of reasoning, but we find little of it in the greatest era of Chinese culture—the T'ang Dynasty, which was some twelve hundred years ago. Certainly China has had its great philosophers, but Chinese philosophy was the result of Buddhist philosophy stimulating the Chinese mind. If China had to stand against Buddhism, it had to take Buddhist philosophy and assimilate it into its own body and make it its own blood. The result of this assimilation was Zen—and the work of assimilation was completed by the Sung Dynasty, which followed the T'ang.

The T'ang Dynasty represents the highest point of Chinese culture. With T'ang the Chinese mind developed to its fullest extent, and everything associated with this dynasty represents the flower of the Chinese mind—art, literature, poetry and religion. Zen is one aspect of that golden age.

In the early days of Buddhism in China the monks used to live in the monastery and devote themselves entirely to the practice of *Dhyāna*. They did not eat after midday, but because of its colder climate, this practice had to be changed. They considered it contrary to the spirit of the Buddha's teaching to refuse to adapt themselves to climatic conditions because of a blind reverence for mere formalities and rules devised for people living in the tropics. If we had to follow man-made rules which are only applicable to India, the result would be comic; things have to be adjusted in accordance with circumstances.

Thus while some monasteries adhered to the Indian rules and customs, these monks who desired a Buddhism more after the heart of the Chinese people formed monasteries of their own. These became the Zen monasteries. They undertake all kinds of manual work. They cultivate rice and vegetables and cut trees for fuel. Even now in Japan they follow that custom, and monks are seen doing all kinds of work which is usually left to laymen.

But teaching is carried on while they are engaged in manual work— not necessarily, however, by giving sermons or lecturing on abstruse subjects. Zen teaching is to be carried on in close connection with our daily life. As we walk in the fields, Zen teachings are to be demonstrated and understood—not outside the work, but with the work and in the work. One day a monk came to a master and asked him, "I have been here under you for many years, and my coming to you was expressly to study Buddhism. But so far you have not imparted to me any Buddhist teaching. If this continues, I shall have to leave you to my great regret." The master replied, "In the morning when you come and salute me with 'Good morning!' I salute you back, 'Good morning! How are you?' When you bring me a cup of tea I gratefully drink it. When you do anything else for me I acknowledge it. What other teachings do you want to have from me?"

There is no special teaching—the most ordinary things in our daily life hide some deep meaning that is yet most plain and explicit; only our eyes need to see where there is a meaning. Unless this eye is opened there will be nothing to learn from Zen. Another teacher said, "In Zen there is nothing special except our everyday thought (*shin*—mind-consciousness)." When we give something, someone receives it and is grateful. Everybody is called upon to do acts of kindness and to acknowledge them, and when it is done to forget all about it. That is the way we go on in this world! There is Zen!

If you say anything more about it—philosophical or ethical or anything else—you are not a Zen man or woman. In fact, when we carry on as we do in our everyday life, there is plenty of Zen in that. But an eye is needed—a third eye. We have two eyes to see two sides of things, but there must be a third eye which will see everything at the same time and yet not see anything. That is to understand Zen. Our two eyes see dualistically, and dualism is at the bottom of all the trouble we have gone through. This does not mean that dualism is to be abolished, only that there ought to be a third eye. The important thing is that the two eyes must remain, but at the same time there ought to be another. When I speak according to the ordinary way of talking, I have to say that a third eye is needed, but in fact this third eye is *outside* the two eyes we already have. But again, the third eye is not between or above the two eyes—*the two eyes are the third eye.* I am beginning to philosophize, and when we philosophize we are no more followers of Zen. Therefore Zen people always close their mouths when they are pressed. But that does not mean they cannot say anything.

That which is not mind nor matter is not Buddha nor anything else. The Absolute seems to be something beyond human understanding. But in discussing the Absolute it is no longer Absolute. We say God is everywhere, but we like to put God in Heaven. How can we conceive God as giving rules to us? If God is immanent, God is ourselves. But Zen does not say that God is transcendent or immanent. When you try to comprehend a fact by means of words, the fact disappears. When we use our minds we have to understand things dualistically—either transcendentally or immanently. When I have explained that, there is nothing more to say. All that is needed is the opening of the third eye. When we have a third eye, it does not annihilate the two eyes. So the world of dualities is not annihilated at all.

Let me tell you a Zen story about this. It is a sort of joke. Yejaku called on Yenen, and asked, "What is your name?" Yenen replied, "Yejaku." Yejaku said, "But that's my own name." Then Yenen said,

"My name is Yenen." Whereupon Yejaku gave a hearty laugh. You are I, and I am you; in oneness there is manyness, and in manyness there is oneness. The transcendental and the immanent God exist at the same time. When they exist at the same time, you cannot say anything about them (i.e., affirm or deny one or the other)—the only thing is to laugh.

You are you and I am I, but at the same time you are not me and I am not you. This particularization cannot be analyzed. So when things are brought to you, you just accept them and say thank you, but do not talk about it. This is the Zen attitude. Zen tries to make you accept things, and when you have accepted them you give a hearty laugh.

# The Threefold Question in Zen

The question, "What is Zen?" is at once easy and difficult to answer. It is easy because there is nothing that is not Zen. I lift my finger thus, and there is Zen. I sit in silence all day uttering no words, and there too is Zen. Everything you do or say is Zen, and everything you do not do or say is also Zen. You see the flowers blooming in the garden, you hear birds singing in the woods, and you have Zen there. No words are needed to explain Zen, for you have it already before they are pronounced. The question is asked simply because you did not know that you had Zen in you, with you, and around you; and therefore it is easy to answer.

But from another point of view the very fact that it is easy to answer makes it extremely difficult to give a satisfactory answer to the question, "What is Zen?" For when you already have a thing, and have it all the time, and yet do not know it, it is hard to convince you of the fact. To have a thing and yet not to know is the same as not to have it from the beginning. Where there is no experience, there is no firsthand knowledge. All you know is *about* it and not itself. To make you realize that you have the very thing you are seeking, it will be necessary to get that thing detached from you so that you can see it before your eyes and even grasp it with your hands. But this is most difficult, for the thing which is always with you can by no means be taken away from you for inspection.

It is just like our not seeing our own eyes. We have to get a mirror to do that. But this is not really seeing the eye as it is, as it functions. What the eye sees in the mirror is its reflection, and not itself. According to Eckhart, "The eye with which I see God is the same with which God sees me." In this case, we must get God in order to see ourselves. This is where the difficulty lies. How do we get God?

But this much I think we can say, that Zen is a kind of self-consciousness. I see a table before me. I know that I am the one who sees it, and I am fully conscious of myself experiencing the event. But Zen is not here yet, something more must be added to it, or must be discovered in it, in order to make this event of seeing really Zen. The question is now: what is this something? It is in all likelihood that which turns my eye inside out and sees itself, not as a reflection, but as a kind of superself which is hidden behind the moral and psychological self. I call this discovery spiritual self-consciousness. No amount of explanation will bring you to this form of self-consciousness. It unfolds itself from the depths of consciousness. No hammering at the door from outside will open it—it opens by itself from within.

In spite of this fact, we must do some hammering from outside, although this may be of no avail as the direct and efficient cause of opening. Yet it must be somehow carried on, for without it there will be no opening. Perhaps the door remains wide open all the time, open to welcome us in, and it is we who hesitate before it; someone is needed to push us in. The entering may not be due to the pushing, but when one sees somebody halting before the door, one feels like pushing him in. And I propose to do this kind of helping, and hope that you do your best to step in, that is, to understand what I am going to present to you as to the quiddity of Zen in the plainest and most direct way I can.

Oryo Yenan (Huang-lung-nan), a great Zen master of the Sung dynasty, was anxious to get his disciples to see into the secret of Zen, and proposed the following threefold question:

1. Everybody has his birthplace; where is yours?
2. How is it that my hands resemble those of the Buddha?
3. How is it that my legs resemble those of the donkey?

These perhaps, except the first, are trivial questions, and the last two are even nonsensical. What has Zen to do with my legs and hands? What does it matter if they resemble those of the Buddha or even those of the donkey? But there is no doubt about the master's seriousness and anxious concern for his pupils. What do these "puzzles" signify? When you understand them, you understand Zen.

The first one is trite if you answer, "I come from Tokyo or from London." But if you say, "I come from God" or "I know not whence, nor whither," the question assumes quite a religio-philosophical aspect. Though the master may have proposed it in a worldly way, the question no doubt acquires deep sense according to the frame of mind with which you approach it.

One of the pupils answered, "I had some rice gruel for breakfast and I feel hungry now." The master nodded his approval. In what relationship if any does this statement stand to the question, "Where is your birthplace"? In what way has the pupil's physiology to do with the philosophy of Zen as implied in the master's inquiry? Is the pupil merely making a fool of the master?

From another point of view, the pupil may be said to be just as serious-minded as the master in describing his bodily conditions, because however high-flying a man's idealism, he cannot escape his physics and physiology to which the spirit is most intimately wedded. The spirit, if it is to function at all, must implement itself in one way or another, while matter is not thought and thought is not matter and they are not to be conceived as self-identical; the one is always so inevitably associated with the other that we cannot cover them in our actual experience. The condition of the stomach decidedly affects the spirit. Did the pupil refer to this fact?

From whatever unknown region a man may have come to this world, the one most assured event is that he is here, and feels hungry at this moment. This experience we can say, therefore, is the sole reality; besides this absolute present there is no whence, no whither. In fact, all the past and the future are perfectly merged in this present moment, which is describable in human terms as hungry or thirsty or painful. Did the pupil survey the master's question from this point of view, and did the master appraise the pupil accordingly? Is this intended to explain what Zen is? Does this understanding of the present in its absolute aspect constitute Zen? I came somewhere in my recent reading across the phrase "the still point of the turning world" referring to the transcendental quality of the present. Does Zen stand at this still point where the past and the future converge? The ancient philosopher speaks of the "unmoved mover." Is the Zen student's consciousness of hunger this unmoved mover?

Everything in this world is subject to change, there is nothing here that is steady, permanent, and will retain its self-identity through its earthly career. This has been declared by the Buddha and other thinkers and is what we call experience. And yet, we all yearn after things immortal, things never moving, and never moved. Where do we get this idea of immovability or eternal quiescence if all that we see around us is forever changing? How do we solve this contradiction:

permanency and changeability, eternity and momentariness, immortality and dying every minute? There must be some way out.

One way we Buddhists think of it is this: Where we are experiencing the fleeting world, we are simultaneously experiencing "one moment, one and infinite"; that is to say, we are able to be conscious of a world of changes because those changes are the very thing that never suffers change. For this reason our consciousness of change and impermanency is deeply interfused with an unconscious consciousness of eternity, unchangeability or timelessness. This interfusion of consciousness and unconsciousness or, in Buddhist terminology, of the Many and the One, of Form *(rūpam)* and Emptiness *(śūnyatā)*, the Distinction (or Discrimination) and Non-distinction (or Non-discrimination) is, we can say, the philosophy of Zen.

If this be so, we may ask, how is it that none of us understand Zen even when we are hungry and conscious of the fact? The answer is that my just being conscious of hunger does not constitute Zen; there must be along with the physiological or psychological consciousness, another form of consciousness, which is a sort of unconsciousness but not in the ordinary sense of the term. For this unconscious consciousness we have no suitable logical or metaphysical term, for the terms used in the various fields of human understanding belong to the order of relativity, and when they are applied to the experience specifically Zen, Zen is liable to be grossly misunderstood. It is due to this reason that Zen literature abounds with superficially meaningless jargon as well as paradoxical and contradictory expressions.

Kokyu Shoryu (Nu-ch'in Shao-lung), was a great Zen master of the Sung dynasty. While still in his tutelage, he entered the master's room and the master said:

> When you say you see it,
> This seeing is not the (true) seeing;
> The (true) seeing is not seeing,
> Seeing can never reach it.

So saying, the master raised his fist and asked, "Do you see?"
Said the disciple, "I see."
"You are putting another head over your own."
Hearing this, the disciple became conscious of something inwardly awakened.

The master observed this and said, "What do you see?"

The disciple did not say this time, "I see," but quoted the poetic passage, "Even when the bamboos are growing thick, they do not obstruct the running stream."

What, let me ask, have they, master and disciple been talking about here? Evidently, speaking Zen-wise, seeing is not seeing, to be conscious is not to be conscious; when you say you have it, you miss it. But the reverse does not hold true, for not-seeing is not at all seeing. There must be actual seeing on the physical plane, and over and through this seeing there must be another sort of seeing, which makes the ordinary seeing a true seeing—which is seeing in the Zen sense.

Let me remark, *en passant,* that what distinguishes the Zen way of seeing or understanding experience from that of the Indian philosophers is generally that Zen speaks of it more in terms of time than those of space. Zen has no doubt developed from Indian thought and is deeply tinged with it, but the Chinese mind has added to it something of its own, and the result is Zen.

A modern thinker, Dr. Radhakrishnan, writes in *The Hibbert Journal* (July 1946):

The whole hierarchy of objective being is dependent on the primary reality, which is therefore both transcendent to it and immanent in it. It is consciousness of self and constitutive of what is other than self. It is the "unmoved mover," the immanent principle in the moving and the unmoving though himself is devoid of any movement. When we look upon the Supreme as the immanent Lord, he becomes the Divine Creator. When the Supreme Spirit objectifies itself thus, the essential unconditional freedom of the spirit becomes involved in conditions and limitations which contradict his freedom.

This is all well as far as it goes, but when he refers to "the Supreme" or "the Divine Creator," it is apt to make us think of something spatially extending. Of course, this is an illusion, and Radhakrishnan is anxious not to have us fall into this intellectual pit, for he says that "the inward self" is beyond the reach of discursive thought and the possibility of conceptual interpretation. In spite of this warning his terminology savors of spatiality. Zen avoids all argumentation; it simply raises a finger and asks, "Do you see?" When one says "Yes," Zen declares, "Don't put another head over the one you already have." When the master asks about the whence of one's being, he is dangerously near the battlefield of absolute reasoning. But the disciple knew how not to step into the hell-fire, and declares, "I had some rice gruel in early morning and am now hungry." He does not say, "I am a manifestation, however imperfect, of the absolute spirit which is above all distinctions." Nor does he say, "I am a concrete reflection of the eternal reason which is immanent in the endless variety of the physical world." Nor does he say, "I am one with the Supreme, the son of God, the only begotten son of God." If all religious teaching is meant to free us from ignorance and corruption, Zen must be said to point to the most direct way of emancipation.

We now come to the second and third question proposed by the Zen master at the beginning of this paper: "Why are my hands like those of the Buddha, and my legs like those of the donkey?" These two questions are practically the same. To the second the disciple put down this, "Under the moon I hear some one playing a lute"; and to the third, "A white crane is standing in the snow hardly distinguishable in color."

Superficially or intellectually judging, these statements have no internal or logical connection with the questions. When it is asked why my hands look like those of the Buddha, or why my legs look like those of the donkey, we may expect some biological or metaphysical or even spiritual analysis. The disciple's answer is no answer according to our every day way of thinking; there is apparently nothing that will satisfy one's intellectual curiosity. In fact, we detect a degenerating tendency in these poetical allusions to the lute playing under the moon, and to the standing crane in the snow, which has turned Zen into a kind of handbook of flowery literary diction. But to those who know what is really intended here, this is expressive enough; there is no ambiguity in them.

The questions in regard to my hands resembling those of the Buddha and my legs those of the donkey have deep metaphysical implications. The questioner does not just request the reason for resemblance in any outward form. He wants you to have attained a spiritual insight into the suchness of being. The main idea the questioner has in mind here is to make us look into our own self and perceive "the still point of the turning world," or lay hand on the moving of the unmoved mover.

When the second question is understood the third solves itself, and my statements hereafter will be confined to the hands. When man learned how to free the hands from supporting the body and began to walk the earth with a pair of legs only, he achieved epoch-making progress in the history of intellectual evolution. The free use of hands means our ability of working on environment. Man can now have his aspirations realized in the objective world. His hands or arms are the tools wherewith this wonder can be accomplished. Before he could swing his arms freely and grasp things with his hands for closer inspection and ready handling, he was a slave to the environment in which he happened to be. He had to make the best of his front paws, along with his locomotive facilities. He was hardly more than an automaton, with no means of expressing himself. Now that he has a pair of free hands with flexible fingers, he can gather up a bouquet of flowers and offer it to the Buddha; he can take up a lute and give vent to his emotion in the moonlight night; he can excavate a huge rock and carve it out into a form of beauty. Becoming an independent actor and creator, has he not now generated a consciousness altogether unique, which is, however, of the same order as the one possessed by the creator of the world? This consciousness or unconscious consciousness cannot be the mere consciousness of vitality, the pure feeling of joy, or anything connected with animality. For "acting" in the human sense and "creating" a new world as *homo faber* has something in it in communion with the working of the divine mind when it commanded, "Let there be light."

Some may remark, there is no comparison possible between divine work and human action, and it is highly sacrilegious even to think of such comparison. But this objection forgets the fact or rather the truth that man was made in the divine image and that this image has the remotest possible relation to outwardness, this-worldliness, or materiality. To be at all divine for an image bearing the name, it must be so in essence, in spirituality. God cannot be thought as being in the possession of hands, arms and legs. God did not mould this universe with all kinds of beings in it with his physical hands and fingers; he created all these things from "nothing," and in all probability our human way of regarding this world as objective reality is an illusion. It may be "nothing," mere "Emptiness" as Buddhists assert, reflecting the original "nothing" out of which God is said to have created the world. However this may be, I now take up the lute and strike on its strings and you hear a certain melody issuing from them. Is this sensuous hearing all that there is in our divine-human consciousness? If so, man as God's image cannot mean anything. Where is he to be distinguished from mere animality? Can there not be something more here, where our minds are attuned to the Divine Mind, a kind of superconsciousness transcending our ordinary sensuous limited consciousness which functions on the plane of psychology? Is this not a superconsciousness, which is frequently designated by Buddhists as "mindlessness" or "thoughtlessness" or "unconscious consciousness"! And is it not this that constitutes the divine-human mind?

The superconsciousness which is possessed by every human being as long as he is created in God's image cannot be separable from the relative sensuous consciousness which performs most useful functions in this world of particulars. The superconsciousness must be thoroughly and in the most perfect manner interfused with the one in daily use; otherwise, the superconsciousness cannot be of any significance to us.

It is indeed so interfused with our psychological consciousness that we are utterly unconscious of its presence. It requires certain spiritual training to be awakened to it, and it is Zen that has for the first time in the world history of mental evolution pointed out this fact. In a word, it is Zen that has become aware of the truth of superconsciousness in connection with the most commonplace doings in our daily life. People generally conceive of things spiritual as going beyond our prosaic everyday experience. But the plainest truth is that everything we experience is saturated, interfused, interpenetrated with spiritual signification, and for this reason my handling the lute, my standing in the snow, my feeling hungry or thirsty after a hard day's work, is surcharged with superconsciousness, with unconscious consciousness.

In conclusion, which is really no conclusion, I wish to quote three Chinese poems which purpose to interpret the meaning of the threefold question which was made the subject of this paper. They were composed by one of the disciples of Oryo Yenan, the author of the question.

Oryo the old master
Has the story of "birthplace";
I know him thoroughly well.
I'll show him up today,
I'll show him up for you:
The cat knows how to catch the old rat.

The Persian merchant arrives in China from the southern seas:
Wherever he comes across special treasures, he will assess them:
Sometimes he pays well, sometimes he gets them cheap;
[Thus trading] he watches the afternoon shadows lengthening as
the sun reaches the western hills.

In summer days we all use the fan,
When winter comes charcoal is heaped in the fireplace to burn:
When you know well what all this means,
Your ignorance stored up for countless *kalpas* melts away.

# Aspects of Japanese Culture

1

When we look at the development of Japanese culture we find that Zen Buddhism has made many important contributions. The other schools of Buddhism have limited their sphere of influence almost entirely to the spiritual life of the Japanese people; but Zen has gone beyond it. Zen has entered internally into every phase of the cultural life of the people.

In China this was not necessarily the case. Zen united itself to a great extent with Taoist beliefs and practices and with the Confucian teaching of morality, but it did not affect the cultural life of the people so much as it did in Japan. (Is it due to the racial psychology of the Japanese people that they have taken up Zen so intensely and deeply that is has entered intimately into their life?) In China, however, I ought not omit to mention the noteworthy fact that Zen gave great impetus to the development of Chinese philosophy in the Sung dynasty and also to the growth of a certain school of painting. A large number of examples of this school were brought over to Japan beginning with the Kamakura era in the thirteenth century, when Zen monks were constantly traveling between the two neighboring countries. The paintings of Southern Sung thus came to find their ardent admirers on our side of the sea and are now national treasures of Japan, while in China no specimens of this class of painting are to be found.

Before proceeding further, we may make a few general remarks about one of the peculiar features of Japanese art, which is closely related to and finally deducible from the world conception of Zen.

Among things which strongly characterized Japanese artistic talents we may mention the so-called "one-corner" style, which originated with Bayen (Ma Yüan *fl.* 1175-1225), one of the greatest Southern Sung artists. The "one-corner" style is psychologically associated with the

Japanese painters' "thrifty brush" tradition of retaining the least possible number of lines or strokes which go to represent forms on silk or paper. Both are very much in accord with the spirit of Zen. A simple fishing boat in the midst of the rippling waters is enough to awaken in the mind of the beholder a sense of the vastness of the sea and at the same time of peace and contentment—the Zen sense of the Alone. Apparently the boat floats helplessly. It is a primitive structure with no mechanical device for stability and for audacious steering over the turbulent waves, with no scientific apparatus for braving all kinds of weather—quite a contrast to the modern ocean liner. But this very helplessness is the virtue of the fishing canoe, in contrast with which we feel the incomprehensibility of the Absolute encompassing the boat and all the world. Again, a solitary bird on a dead branch, in which not a line, not a shade, is wasted, is enough to show us the loneliness of autumn, when days become shorter and nature begins to roll up once more its gorgeous display of luxurious summer vegetation.[1] It makes one feel somewhat pensive, but it gives one opportunity to withdraw the attention towards the inner life, which, given attention enough, spreads out its rich treasures ungrudgingly before the eyes.

Here we have an appreciation of transcendental aloofness in the midst of multiplicities—which is known as *wabi* in the dictionary of Japanese cultural terms. *Wabi* really means "poverty," or, negatively, "not to be in the fashionable society of the time." To be poor, that is, not to be dependent on things worldly—wealth, power and reputation— and yet to feel inwardly the presence of something of the highest value, above time and social position: this is what essentially constitutes *wabi*. Stated in terms of practical everyday life, *wabi* is to be satisfied with a little hut, a room of two or three *tatami* (mats), like the log cabin of Thoreau, and with a dish of vegetables picked in the neighboring fields, and perhaps to be listening to the pattering of a gentle spring rainfall. The cult of *wabi* has entered deeply into the cultural life of the Japanese people. It is in truth the worshiping of poverty—probably a most appropriate cult in a poor country like ours. Despite the modern Western luxuries and comforts of life which have invaded us, there is still an ineradicable longing in us for the cult of *wabi*. Even in the intellectual life, not richness of ideas, not brilliancy or solemnity in

[1]For pictures of a similar nature, see my *Zen Essays,* II and III.

marshaling thoughts and building up a philosophical system, is sought; but just to stay quietly content with the mystical contemplation of Nature and to feel at home with the world is more inspiring to us, at least to some of us.

However "civilized," however much brought up in an artificially contrived environment, we all seem to have an innate longing for primitive simplicity, close to the natural state of living. Hence the city people's pleasure in summer camping in the woods or traveling in the desert or opening up an unbeaten track. We wish to go back once in a while to the bosom of Nature and feel her pulsation directly. Zen's habit of mind, to break through all forms of human artificiality and take firm hold of what lies behind them, has helped the Japanese not to forget the soil but to be always friendly with Nature and appreciate her unaffected simplicity. Zen has no taste for complexities that lie on the surface of life. Life itself is simple enough, but when it is surveyed by the analyzing intellect it presents unparalleled intricacies. With all the apparatus of science we have not yet fathomed the mysteries of life. But, once in its current, we seem to be able to understand it, with its apparently endless pluralities and entanglements. Very likely, the most characteristic thing in the temperament of the Eastern people is the ability to grasp life from within and not from without. And Zen has just struck it.

In painting especially, disregard of form results when too much attention or emphasis is given to the all-importance of the spirit. The "one-cornered" style and the economy of brush strokes also help to effect aloofness from conventional rules. Where you would ordinarily expect a line or a mass or a balancing element, you miss it, and yet this very thing awakens in you an unexpected feeling of pleasure. In spite of shortcomings or deficiencies that no doubt are apparent, you do not feel them so; indeed, this imperfection itself becomes a form of perfection. Evidently, beauty does not necessarily spell perfection of form. This has been one of the favorite tricks of Japanese artists—to embody beauty in a form of imperfection or even of ugliness.

When this beauty of imperfection is accompanied by antiquity or primitive uncouthness, we have a glimpse of *sabi,* so prized by Japanese connoisseurs. Antiquity and primitiveness may not be an actuality. If an object of art suggests even superficially the feeling of a historical period, there is *sabi* in it. *Sabi* consists in rustic unpretentiousness or archaic imperfection, apparent simplicity or effortlessness in execution, and richness in historical associations (which, however, may not always be present); and lastly, it contains inexplicable elements that raise the object in question to the rank of an artistic production. These elements are generally regarded as derived from the appreciation of Zen. The utensils used in the tearoom are mostly of this nature.

The artistic element that goes into the constitution of *sabi,* which literally means "loneliness" or "solitude," is poetically defined by a teamaster thus:

> As I come out
> To this fishing village,
> Late in the autumn day,
> No flowers in bloom I see,
> Nor any tinted maple leaves.[2]

Aloneness indeed appeals to contemplation and does not lend itself to spectacular demonstration. It may look most miserable, insignificant, and pitiable, especially when it is put up against the Western or modern setting. To be left alone, with no streamers flying, no fireworks crackling, and this amidst a gorgeous display of infinitely varied forms and endlessly changing colors, is indeed no sight at all. Take one of those *sumiye* sketches, perhaps portraying Kanzan and Jittoku (Hanshan and Shi'h-tê),[3] hang it in a European or an American art gallery, and see what effect it will produce in the minds of the visitors. The idea of aloneness belongs to the East and is at home in the environment of its birth.

It is not only to the fishing village on the autumnal eve that aloneness gives form but also to a patch of green in the early spring—which is in all likelihood even more expressive of the idea of *sabi* or *wabi.* For in the green patch, as we read in the following thirty-one-syllable verse, there is an indication of life impulse amidst the wintry desolation:

> To those who only pray for the cherries to bloom,
> How I wish to show the spring
> That gleams from a patch of green
> In the midst of the snow-covered mountain-village![4]

[2]Fujiwara Sadaiye (1162–1241).

[3]Zen poet-recluses of the T'ang dynasty who have been a favorite subject for Far Eastern painters.

[4]Fujiwara Iyetaka (1158-1237).

This is given by one of the old teamasters as thoroughly expressive of *sabi,* which is one of the four principles governing the cult of tea, *cha-no-yu.* Here is just a feeble inception of life power as asserted in the form of a little green patch, but in it he who has an eye can readily discern the spring shooting out from underneath the forbidding snow. It may be said to be a mere suggestion that stirs his mind, but just the same it is life itself and not its feeble indication. To the artist, life is as much here as when the whole field is overlaid with verdure and flowers. One may call this the mystic sense of the artist.

Asymmetry is another feature that distinguishes Japanese art. The idea is doubtlessly derived from the "one-corner" style of Bayen. The plainest and boldest example is the plan of Buddhist architecture. The principal structures, such as the Tower Gate, the Dharma Hall, the Buddha Hall, and others, may be laid along one straight line; but structures of secondary or supplementary importance, sometimes even those of major importance, are not arranged symmetrically as wings along either side of the main line. They may be found irregularly scattered over the grounds in accordance with the topographical peculiarities. You will readily be convinced of this fact if you visit some of the Buddhist temples in the mountains, for example, the Iyeyasu shrine at Nikko. We can say that asymmetry is quite characteristic of Japanese architecture of this class.

This can be demonstrated *par excellence* in the construction of the tearoom and in the tools used in connection with it. Look at the ceiling, which may be constructed in at least three different styles, and at some of the utensils for serving tea, and again at the grouping and laying of the steppingstones or flagstones in the garden. We find so many illustrations of asymmetry, or, in a way, of imperfection, or of the "one-corner" style.

Some Japanese moralists try to explain this liking of the Japanese artists for things asymmetrically formed and counter to the conventional, or rather geometrical, rules of art by the theory that the people have been morally trained not to be obtrusive but always to efface themselves, and that this mental habit of self-annihilation manifests itself accordingly in art—for example, when the artist leaves the important central space unoccupied. But, to my mind, this theory is not quite  correct. Would it not be a more plausible explanation to say that the artistic genius of the Japanese people has been inspired by the Zen way of looking at individual things as perfect in themselves and at the same time as embodying the nature of totality which belongs to the One?

The doctrine of ascetic aestheticism is not so fundamental as that of Zen aestheticism. Art impulses are more primitive or more innate than those of morality. The appeal of art goes more directly into human nature. Morality is regulative, art is creative. One is an imposition from without, the other is an irrepressible expression from within. Zen finds its inevitable association with art but not with morality. Zen may remain unmoral but not without art. When the Japanese artists create objects imperfect from the point of view of form, they may even be willing to ascribe their art motive to the current notion of moral asceticism; but we need not give too much significance to their own interpretation or to that of the critic. Our consciousness is not, after all, a very reliable standard of judgment.

However this may be, asymmetry is certainly characteristic of Japanese art, which is one of the reasons informality or approachability also marks to a certain degree Japanese objects of art. Symmetry inspires a notion of grace, solemnity, and impressiveness, which is again the case with logical formalism or the piling up of abstract ideas. The Japanese are often thought not to be intellectual and philosophical, because their general culture is not thoroughly impregnated with intellectuality. This criticism, I think, results somewhat from the Japanese love of asymmetry. The intellectual primarily aspires to balance, while the Japanese are apt to ignore it and incline strongly towards imbalance.

Imbalance, asymmetry, the "one-corner," poverty, simplification, *sabi* or *wabi,* aloneness, and cognate ideas make up the most conspicuous and characteristic features of Japanese art and culture. All these emanate from one central perception of the truth of Zen, which is "the One in the Many and the Many in the One," or better, "the One remaining as one in the Many individually and collectively."

2

That Zen has helped to stimulate the artistic impulses of the Japanese people and to color their works with ideas characteristic of Zen is due to the following facts: the Zen monasteries were almost exclusively the repositories of learning and art, at least during the Kamakura and the Muromachi eras; the Zen monks had constant opportunities to come in

contact with foreign cultures; the monks themselves were artists, scholars, and mystics; they were even encouraged by the political powers of
the time to engage in commercial enterprises to bring foreign objects of
art and industry to Japan; the aristocrats and the politically influential
classes of Japan were patrons of Zen institutions and were willing to
submit themselves to the discipline of Zen. Zen thus worked not only
directly on the religious life of the Japanese but also most strongly on
their general culture.

The Tendai, the Shingon, and the Jōdō[5] contributed greatly to imbue
the Japanese with the spirit of Buddhism, and through their icon-
ography to develop their artistic instincts for sculpture, color paintings,
architecture, textile fabrics, and metalwork. But the philosophy of
Tendai is too abstract and abstruse to be understood by the masses; the
ritualism of Shingon is too elaborate and complicated and consequently too expensive for popularity. On the other hand, Shingon and
Tendai and Jōdō produced fine sculpture and pictures and artistic utensils to be used in their daily worship. The most highly prized "national
treasures" belong to the Tempyō, the Nara, and the Heian periods,
when those two schools of Buddhism were in the ascendency and
intimately involved with the cultured classes of the people. The Jōdō
teaches the Pure Land in all its magnificence, where the Buddha of
Infinite Light is attended by his retinue of Bodhisattvas, and this
inspired the artists to paint those splendid pictures of Amida preserved
in the various Buddhist temples of Japan. The Nichiren and the Shin
are the creation of the Japanese religious mind. The Nichiren gave no
specifically artistic and cultural impetus to us; the Shin tended to be
somewhat iconoclastic and produced nothing worth mentioning in the
arts and literature except the hymns known as *wasan* and the "honor-
able letters" *(gobunsho* or *ofumi)* chiefly written by Rennyo
(1415–99).

Zen came to Japan after Shingon and Tendai and was at once
embraced by the military classes. It was more or less by an historical
accident that Zen was set against the aristocratic priesthood. The
nobility, too, in the beginning felt a certain dislike for it and made use of
their political advantage to stir up opposition to Zen. In the beginning

[5]These, with the Shin and the Nichiren, are the principal schools of Buddhism
in Japan.

of the Japanese history of Zen, therefore, Zen avoided Kyoto and established itself under the patronage of the Hōjō family in Kamakura. This place, as the seat of the feudal government in those days, became the headquarters of Zen discipline. Many Zen monks from China settled in Kamakura and found strong support in the Hōjō family— Tokiyori, Tokimune, and their successors and retainers.

The Chinese masters brought many artists and objects of art along with them, and the Japanese who came back from China were also bearers of art and literature. Pictures of Kakei (Hsia Kuei, *fl.* (1190–1220), Mokkei (Mu-ch'i, *fl. c.* 1240), Ryōkai (Liang K'ai, *fl. c.* 1210), Bayen (Ma Yüan, *fl.* 1175–1225), and others thus found their way to Japan. Manuscripts of the noted Zen masters of China were also given shelter in the monasteries here. Calligraphy in the Far East is an art just as much as *sumiye* painting, and it was cultivated almost universally among the intellectual classes in olden times. The spirit pervading Zen pictures and calligraphy made a strong impression on them, and Zen was readily taken up and followed. In it there is something virile and unbending. A mild, gentle, and graceful air—almost feminine, one might call it—which prevailed in the periods preceding the Kamakura, is now superseded by an air of masculinity, expressing itself mostly in the sculpture and calligraphy of the period. The rugged virility of the warriors of the Kwanto districts is proverbial, in contrast to the grace and refinement of the courtiers in Kyoto. The soldierly quality, with its mysticism and aloofness from worldly affairs, appeals to the willpower. Zen in this respect walks hand in hand with the spirit of Bushido ("Warriors' Way").

Another factor in the discipline of Zen, or rather in the monastic life in which Zen carries out its scheme of teaching, is this: as the monastery is usually situated in the mountains, its inmates are in the most intimate touch with nature, they are close and sympathetic students of it. They observe plants, birds, animals, rocks, rivers which people of the town would leave unnoticed. And their observation deeply reflects their philosophy, or better, their intuition. It is not that of a mere naturalist. It penetrates into the life itself of the objects that come under the monks' observation. Whatever they may paint of nature will inevitably be expressive of this intuition; the "spirit of the mountains" will be felt softly breathing in their works.

The fundamental intuition the Zen masters gain through their discipline seems to stir up their artistic instincts if they are at all susceptible to art. The intuition that impels the masters to create beautiful things, that is, to express the sense of perfection through things ugly and imperfect, is apparently closely related to the feeling for art. The Zen masters may not make good philosophers, but they are very frequently fine artists. Even their technique is often of the first order, and besides they know how to tell us something unique and original. One such is Musō the National Teacher (1275–1351). He was a fine calligrapher and a great landscape gardener; wherever he resided, at quite a number of places in Japan, he designed splendid gardens, some of which are still in existence and well preserved after so many years of changing times. Among the noted painters of Zen in the fourteenth and fifteenth centuries we may mention Chō Densu (d. 1431), Kei Shoki (*fl.* 1490), Josetsu (*fl.* 1375–1420), Shūbun (*fl.* 1420–50), Seshū (1421–1506), and others.

Georges Duthuit, the author of *Chinese Mysticism and Modern Painting,* seems to understand the spirit of Zen mysticism. From him we have this: "When the Chinese artist paints, what matters is the concentration of thought and the prompt and vigorous response of the hand to the directing will. Tradition ordains him to see, or rather to feel, as a whole the work to be executed, before embarking on anything. 'If the ideas of a man are confused, he will become the slave of exterior conditions.' . . . He who deliberates and moves his brush intent on making a picture, misses to a still greater extent the art of painting. [This seems like a kind of automatic writing.] Draw bamboos for ten years, become a bamboo, then forget all about bamboos when you are drawing. In possession of an infallible technique, the individual places himself at the mercy of inspiration."

To become a bamboo and to forget that you are one with it while drawing it—this is the Zen of the bamboo, this is the moving with the "rhythmic movement of the spirit" which resides in the bamboo as well as in the artist himself. What is now required of him is to have a firm hold on the spirit and yet not to be conscious of the fact. This is a very difficult task achieved only after long spiritual training.[6] The Eastern people have been taught since the earliest times to subject themselves to

[6]Cf. Takuan on "Prajñā Immovable."

this kind of discipline if they want to achieve something in the world of art and religion. Zen, in fact, has given expression to it in the following phrase: "One in All and All in One." When this is thoroughly understood, there is creative genius.

It is of utmost importance here to interpret the phrase in its proper sense. People imagine that it means pantheism, and some students of Zen seem to agree. This is to be regretted, for pantheism is something foreign to Zen and also to the artist's understanding of his work. When the Zen masters declare the One to be in the All and the All in the One, they do not mean that the one is the other and *vice versa*. As the One is in the All, some people suppose that Zen is a pantheistic teaching. Far from it; Zen would never hypostatize the One or the All as a thing to be grasped by the sense. The phrase "One in All and All in One" is to be understood as an expression of absolute *Prajñā*-intuition and is not to be conceptually analyzed. When we see the moon, we know that it is the moon, and that is enough. Those who proceed to analyze the experience and try to establish a theory of knowledge are not students of Zen. They cease to be so, if they ever were, at the very moment of their procedure as analysts. Zen always upholds its experience as such and refuses to commit itself to any system of philosophy.

Even when Zen indulges in intellection, it never subscribes to a pantheistic interpretation of the world. For one thing, there is no One in Zen. If Zen ever speaks of the One as if it recognized it, this is a kind of condescension to common parlance. To Zen students, the One is the All and the All is the One; and yet the One remains the One and the All the All. "Not two!" may lead the logician to think, "It is One." But the master would go on, saying, "Not One either!" "What then?" we may ask. We here face a blind alley, as far as verbalism is concerned. Therefore, it is said that "If you wish to be in direct communion [with Reality], I tell you 'Not two!'"

The following *mondo*[7] may help to illustrate the point I wish to make in regard to the Zen attitude towards the so-called pantheistic interpretation of nature.

A monk asked Tōsu (T'ou-tzu), a Zen master of the T'ang period: "I understand that all sounds are the voice of the Buddha. Is this right?" The master said, "That is right." The monk then proceeded: "Would

[7]This and what follows are all from the *Hekigan-shu*, case 79.

not the master please stop making a noise which echoes the sound of a fermenting mass of filth?" The master thereupon struck the monk.

The monk further asked Tōsu: "Am I in the right when I understand the Buddha as asserting that all talk, however trivial or derogatory, belongs to ultimate truth?" The master said, "Yes, you are in the right." The monk went on, "May I then call you a donkey?" The master thereupon struck him.

It may be necessary to explain these *mondo* in plain language. To conceive every sound, every noise, every utterance one makes as issuing from the fountainhead of one Reality, that is, from one God, is pantheistic, I imagine. For "he giveth to all life, and breath, and all things" (Acts 17:25); and again, "For in him we live, and move, and have our being" (Acts 17:28). If this be the case, a Zen master's hoarse throat echoes the melodious resonance of the voice flowing from the Buddha's golden mouth, and even when a great teacher is decried as reminding one of an ass, the defamation must be regarded as reflecting something of ultimate truth. All forms of evil must be said somehow to be embodying what is true and good and beautiful, and to be a contribution to the perfection of Reality. To state it more concretely, bad is good, ugly is beautiful, false is true, imperfect is perfect, and also conversely. This is, indeed, the kind of reasoning in which those indulge who conceive the God-nature to be immanent in all things. Let us see how the Zen master treats this problem.

It is remarkable that Tōsu put his foot right down against such intellectualist interpretations and struck his monk. The latter in all probability expected to see the master nonplussed by his statements which logically follow from his first assertion. The masterful Tōsu knew, as all Zen masters do, the uselessness of making any verbal demonstration against such a "logician." For verbalism leads from one complication to another; there is no end to it. The only effective way, perhaps, to make such a monk as this one realize the falsehood of his conceptual understanding is to strike him and so let him experience within himself the meaning of the statement, "One in All and All in One." The monk was to be awakened from his logical somnambulism. Hence Tōsu's drastic measure.

Secchō here gives his comments in the following lines:

Pity that people without number try to play with the tide;        3.
They are all ultimately swallowed up into it and die!
Let them suddenly awake [from the deadlock],
And see that all the rivers run backward, swelling and surging.[8]

What is needed here is an abrupt turning or awakening, with which        4,
one comes to the realization of the truth of Zen—which is neither
transcendentalism nor immanentism nor a combination of the two.
The truth is as Tōsu declares in the following:        4.
A monk asks, "What is the Buddha?"
Tōsu answers, "The Buddha."
Monk: "What is the Tao?"
Tōsu: "The Tao."
Monk: "What is Zen?"
Tōsu: "Zen."
The master answers like a parrot, he is echo itself. In fact, there is no
other way of illumining the monk's mind than affirming that what is
is—which is the final fact of experience.
Another example[9] is given to illustrate the point. A monk asked        5.
Jōshu (Chao-chou), of the T'ang dynasty: "It is stated that the Perfect
Way knows no difficulties, only that it abhors discrimination. What is
meant by No-discrimination?"
Jōshu said, "Above the heavens and below the heavens, I alone am
the Honored One."
The monk suggested, "Still a discrimination."
The master's retort was, "O this worthless fellow! Where is the
discrimination?"
By discrimination the Zen masters mean what we have when we
refuse to accept Reality as it is or in its suchness, for we then reflect on it
and analyze it into concepts, going on with intellection and finally
landing on a circulatory reasoning. Jōshu's affirmation is a final one
and allows no equivocation, no argumentation. We have simply to take
it as it stands and remain satisfied with it. In case we somehow fail to do

---

[8]Seccho (Hsüeh-tou, 980–1052) was one of the great Zen masters of the Sung,
noted for his literary accomplishment. The *Hekigan-shu* is based on Seccho's
"One Hundred Cases," which he selected out of the annals of Zen.

[9]*Hekigan-shu,* case 57.

this, we just leave it alone, and go somewhere else to seek our own enlightenment. The monk could not see where Jōshu was, and he went further on and remarked, "This is still a discrimination!" The discrimination in point of fact is on the monk's side and not on Jōshu's. Hence "the Honored One" now turns into "a worthless fellow."

As I said before, the phrase "All in One and One in All" is not to be analyzed first to the concepts "One" and "All," and the preposition is not then to be put between them; no discrimination is to be exercised here, but one is just to accept it and abide with it, which is really no-abiding at all. There is nothing further to do. Hence the master's striking or calling names. He is not indignant, nor is he short-tempered, but he wishes thereby to help his disciples out of the pit which they have dug themselves. No amount of argument avails here, no verbal persuasion. Only the master knows how to turn them away from a logical impasse and how to open a new way for them; let them, therefore, simply follow him. By following him they all come back to their Original Home.

When an intuitive or experiential understanding of Reality is verbally formulated as "All in One and One in All," we have there the fundamental statement as it is taught by all the various schools of Buddhism. In the terminology of the Prajñā school, this is: *śūnyatā* ("Emptiness") is *tathatā* ("Suchness"), and *tathatā* is *śūnyatā: śūnyatā* is the world of the Absolute, and *tathatā* is the world of particulars. One of the commonest sayings in Zen is "Willows are green and flowers red" or "Bamboos are straight and pine trees are gnarled." Facts of experience are accepted as they are, Zen is not nihilistic, nor is it merely positivistic. Zen would say that just because the bamboo is straight it is of Emptiness, or that just because of Emptiness the bamboo cannot be anything else but a bamboo and not a pine tree. What makes the Zen statements different from mere sense experience, however, is that Zen's intuition grows out of *Prajñā* and not out of *jñā*.[10] It is from this point of view that when asked "What is Zen?" the master sometimes answers "Zen" and sometimes "Not-Zen."

---

[10] *Prajñā* may be translated "transcendental wisdom," while *jñā* or *vijñāna* is "relative knowledge." For a detailed explanation, see my *Studies in Zen Buddhism*, pp. 85 ff.

We can see now that the principle of *sumiye* painting is derived from this Zen experience, and that directness, simplicity, movement spirituality, completeness, and other qualities we observe in the *sumiye* class of Oriental paintings have organic relationship to Zen. There is no pantheism in *sumiye* as there is none in Zen.

There is another thing I must not forget to mention in this connection, which is perhaps the most important factor in *sumiye* as well as in Zen. It is creativity. When it is said that *sumiye* depicts the spirit of an object, or that it gives a form to what has no form, this means that there must be a spirit of creativity moving over the picture. The painter's business thus is not just to copy or imitate nature, but to give to the object something living in its own right. It is the same with the Zen master. When he says that the willow is green and the flower is red, he is not just giving us a description of how nature looks, but something whereby green is green and red is red. This something is what I call the spirit of creativity. *Śūnyatā* is formless, but it is the fountainhead of all possibilities. To turn what is possible into an actuality is an act of creativity. When Tōsu is asked, "What is Dharma?" he answers, "Dharma"; when asked "What is Buddha?" he answers, "Buddha." This is by no means a parrotlike response, a mere echoing; all the answers come out of his creative mind, without which there is no Zen in Tōsu. The understanding of Zen is to understand what kind of mind this is. Yakusan's meeting with Rikō will illustrate this.[11]

Yakusan (Yao-shan, 751–834) was a great master of the T'ang era. When Rikō (Li Ao), governor of the province, heard of his Zen mastership, he sent for him to come to the capital. Yakusan, however, refused to come. This happened several times. Rikō grew impatient and came in person to see the master in his own mountain retreat. Yakusan was reading the *sūtras* and paid no attention whatever to the arrival of the governor. The attendant monk reminded the master of the fact, but he still kept on reading. Rikō felt hurt and remarked, "Seeing the face is not at all like hearing the name." By this he meant that the person in actuality was not equal to his reputation. Yakusan called out, "O Governor!" Rikō echoed at once, "Yes, Master." The master then said,

[11] *Dentō-roku* ("Transmission of the Lamp"), fasc. 14.

"Why do you evaluate the hearing over the seeing?" The governor apologized and asked, "What is Tao?" Yakusan pointed up with his hand and then down, and said, "Do you understand?" Rikō said, "No, Master." Thereupon Yakusan remarked, "The clouds are in the sky and water in the jar." It is said that this pleased the governor very much.

Did Rikō really understand what Yakusan meant? Yakusan's is no more than a plain statement of facts as they are, and we may ask, "Where is Tao?" Rikō was a great scholar and philosopher. He must have had some abstract conception of Tao. Could he so readily reconcile his view with Yakusan's? Whatever we may say about this, Yakusan and Tōsu and other Zen masters are all walking the same track. The artists are also required to strike it.

# Zen and Japanese Art

## 1

There must be something in Japanese character that harmonizes well with the spirit of Zen, for the latter has so readily and thoroughly been merged in the life and culture of the Japanese people that we can recognize its presence there, though not always in a uniform way. Its introduction into Japan took place in the Kamakura era.

Zen first united itself with the spirit of Samurai as soon as it gained its foothold in the Land of the Rising Sun. The Hōzyō family built several Zen temples in Kamakura, and their leaders most earnestly studied Zen under the teachers from China. Naturally the knights serving the Hōzyō government followed the example. Their resolute and almost reckless deeds of bravery are recorded in the annals of those days.

It was not, however, until the Asikaga era that Zen's spiritual influence permeated through the various fields of art so as to effect the general life of the people.

## 2

Among the most remarkable features characterizing Zen we find these: spirituality, directness of expression, disregard of form or conventionalism, and frequently an almost wanton delight in going astray from respectability. For instance, when form requires a systematic treatment of the subject in question, a Zen painter may wipe out every trace of such and let an insignificant piece of rock occupy just one corner of the field. Where absolute cleanliness is the thing sought after, a Zen gardener may have a few dead leaves scattered over the garden. A Zen sword-player may stand in an almost nonchalant attitude before the foe as if the latter can strike him in any way he liked; but when he actually tries his best, the Zen man would over-awe him with his very unconcernedness. In these respects, Zen is unexpectedness itself, it is beyond logical or common-sense calculation.

3

The main reason for Zen's unexpectedness or incalculability comes from its transcending conceptualization. It expresses itself in the most impossible or irrational manner; it does not allow anything to stand between itself and its expression. In fact, the only thing that limits Zen is its wanting to express itself. But this limitation is imposed upon everything human and indeed upon things divine as long as these are to be made intelligible.

The spirit of Zen is then the going beyond conceptualization, and this means to grasp the spirit of the most intimate manner. This in turn means the disregarding to a certain extent of all technique. The idea may better be expressed by stating that Zen holds in itself something which eludes all systematized technical skill but which is to be somehow grasped in order to come in the closest possible touch with Life, all-generating and all-pervading and all-invigorating.

4

The chief concern of the Japanese artist is to stand in an intimate relationship with this Life, this Spirit. Even when he has mastered all the technique necessary for the profession, he will not stop there, for he still finds himself wanting; he is still under the bondage of the technical restrictions and traditionalism; his creative genius he feels somehow clamped; he fails to give it the freest possible expressions. He has spent so many years to quality himself as a worthy heir to his profession, laden with a line of brilliant masters, but his works are not short of his ideals, they are not precipitating with Life, that is to say, he is not satisfied with himself—he is not a creator, but an imitator.

When the Japanese artist reaches this stage, he frequently knocks at the gate of a Zen master. He asks the latter to lead him to the inner sanctuary of Zen. When Zen is understood, the spirit takes varied form for its expression: the painter expresses it in paintings, the sculptor in sculptures, the Noh-dancer in dancing, the tea-master in tea-cult, the gardener in gardening, and so on.

5

One of the Kanō masters was asked to paint a dragon on the ceiling of one of the main buildings belonging to Myōsinzi. He wished to make it one of his masterpieces, for the temple lives long and is generally a repository of all kinds of great works of art. But he did not quite feel equal to the task. The dragon is of course a mythical creature, and the painter was naturally not ambitious to make his work look like a genuine one. His desire was to create it out of his own imagination full of life and spirit so that the animal however grotesque in appearance would be the painter himself living in a world of ideas. To achieve this was no easy task. The reality of sense incessantly worked against him as he wished to fly away to a heaven of artistic fantasies. The painter finally came to the abbot of the monastery who was a great Zen master of the day, and asked him how to proceed in his work. The master simply said, "You be the dragon yourself." The Kanō artist did not know how to take this advice, but after much cogitation the idea dawned on him. When he finally came back to the master, he was no more the plain painter who was trying to paint a dragon, he was the dragon himself. The master then told him to go ahead with his work. The work was the dragon painting himself, and not a human artist trying to portray the mythical creature. The work can still be seen on the original ceiling as the painter painted it in black and white.

6

An asymmetrical treatment of a subject is characteristically Zen as well as Japanese. One often comes across a square or circle cut off at one corner, a tea-cup quite disfigured, a dinner tray covered with dishes of varied shape, or a room with ceilings of different designs and with windows of various sizes and shapes cut into the walls. The typical example of asymmetry is the tea-room.

Asymmetry may be considered an imperfection, but in my view this is not true. A broken line is just as artistically perfect as a straight line or a curve. It all depends where one would fix a standard. A broken line or an irregular curve is perfect in its very "imperfection." If it is made to serve a utilitarian purpose a curve or line is to be perfectly formed, but art has no such teleology. This freedom from teleology is the spirit of Zen as well as of art.

7

A broken line or an imperfect representation of an object may be
regarded as suggesting something regularly and therefore perfectly
shaped; but from the Zen point of view which is also the Japanese way
of feeling, a thing however misshaped is perfect and artistic in its being
misshaped. What is needed here to make an imperfection perfect is the
presence of the artist's spiritual love for the object—a love which is
above egotism but which issues from Great Spirit.

8

The Japanese people are noted for their liking small things and
making big things of them. This has a historical background but in
reality it reflects the spirit of Zen, which turns the Buddha sixteen feet
high into a single blade of grass and the latter into the former, and
which also takes in a seed of mustard the great peak of Mount Sumeru.
An insignificant green frog sits on a lotus leaf an early summer morning
in a garden pond surrounded by some luxuriantly growing trees. A
painter takes up this creature on a piece of silk and makes it sit on the
lotus as if it were enjoying a life in the Pure Land. There it altogether
loses is insignificance; it looks about it contented with itself; the leaf
may occasionally be shaken by a gentle breeze, but it knows where it is
and securely balances itself, taking all things in as if all belonged to it or
as if it were one with them. It is after all not the frog that is rested there
but the painter himself who is satisfied with himself and the
world—no, it is not the painter himself, it is even the Great Spirit of
the Universe. Not only the artist but the onlooker also is absorbed
into the spirit pervading the picture.

This wonderful transformation realized through the agency of a little
green summer frog has really taken place owing to the Zen-painter's
loving spirit which embraces the world and all.

9

What a Zen-artist actually performs is not to suggest what is omitted,
but to make the whole reality reflect itself in the small things before
ourselves. For when the latter are understood they present themselves
to be more than themselves. They are realities and not mere suggestions

of them. Before Zen took hold of the Japanese soul, this was not possible however much of this proclivity there was in it. It will not express itself in this way. Zen made it eloquent and it ceased to be dumb. The primitive mind may harbor many virtues and possibilities deeply buried underneath, but it requires a touch of a higher spiritual culture which brings them out to the front through stages of historical development. Zen has fulfilled this requirement for the Japanese soul.

# Rinzai on Zen
## TRANSLATION FROM THE CHINESE
## AND COMMENTARY

What follows is the first English translation of a sermon from the *Sayings of Rinzai (Lin-chi Lu)*. Rinzai (Lin-chi), who died in 867, was a prominent master of the T'ang dynasty (618–905), and the school of Zen that started after him bears his name. His sermons and other material containing his "life" and *mondo* (questions and answers) were compiled after his death by a chief disciple, and the sermon reproduced here is probably one of Rinzai's first expository utterances on Zen. The *Sayings,* a book of about 14,800 characters, is considered one of the most remarkable documents elucidating the principles of Zen. Those who study Zen in one way or another cannot afford to neglect it.

The following points may be enumerated as characterizing the thought of Rinzai: (1) true understanding, (2) freedom, (3) not being deluded by others, (4) faith in self, (5) not craving for externalities, (6) "the one who is at this moment listening to my sermon," (7) nothing wanting in each of us, (8) a man of *buji,* and (9) not being different from the Buddha.

The master then said:

Those of you who wish to discipline themselves in Buddha's Dharma[1] must seek true understanding. When this understanding is attained you will not be defiled by birth and death.[2] Whether walking or standing still, you will be your own master.[3] Even when you are not trying to achieve something extraordinary,[4] it will come to you all by itself.

O Followers of the Way, from olden times each of my predecessors had his own way of training his disciples. As to my way of leading people: all that they need is not to be deluded by others. [Be independent] and go on your way whenever you desire; have no hesitancy.

Do you know where the disease lies which keeps you learners from reaching [true understanding]? It lies where you have no faith in your Self. When faith in your Self is lacking you find yourself hurried by others in every possible way. At every encounter you are no longer your master; you are driven about by others this way or that.

All that is required is all at once to cease leaving your Self in search of something external. When this is done you will find your Self no different from the Buddha or the patriarch.

Do you want to know who the Buddha or patriarch is? He is no other than the one who is, at this moment, right in front of me, listening to my talk on the Dharma. You have no faith in him and therefore you are in quest of someone else somewhere outside. And what will you find? Nothing but words and names, however excellent. You will never reach the moving spirit in the Buddha or patriarch. Make no mistake.

O Venerable Sirs, do not fail to take advantage of the present life we are enjoying. If you fail, this opportunity may never come again, even for as long as you go on transmigrating through the triple world, assuming one form of existence or another, for hundreds of thousands of *kalpas*. When you keep up your life of pleasures your incarnation in the body of an ass or a cow is an assured fact.

O Followers of the Way, according to my view, I see no difference between myself and Śākyamuni.[5] As I live this life of mine today in response to all kinds of situations, is there anything I am in want of? There is no interruption of light wonderfully emanating from my six senses.[6] When you see how this is, you will be no less than men of *buji*[7] all your lives.

O Venerable Sirs, there is no peace in the triple world, it is like a house on fire. It is not a place where you can stay for any length of time. When the devil of impermanence visits you, he does not differentiate between the humble and the noble, between the young and the aged. In no time they are all his prey.

If you desire to be like the Buddha or the patriarch, do not seek anything external. Radiating from the mind at every thought-moment, there is a ray of absolute purity—the *Dharmakāya*[8] in your body; there is a ray of non-discrimination[9]—the *Sambhogakāya* in your body; there is a ray of non-differentiation—the *Nirmāṇakāya* in your body. This triple body[10] is no other than your Self, who is listening at this moment in front of me to my talk on the Dharma. All these activities are revealed when your searching externally ceases.

For scholars of the *sūtras* and *śāstras,*[11] the doctrine of *Trikāya* is the final teaching of the Buddha. But from my point of view the *Trikāya* is nothing but a word—only a triple style of clothes a man may put on.

### NOTES

[1]Dharma *(hō, fa)* has several meanings. Here it is used in the sense of reality, the ultimate, truth, absolute reason, etc.

[2]The cycle of birth and death is *saṃsāra* in Sanskrit. It stands against absolute reason or something that remains eternally in spite of all the vicissitudes that go in this world of relativity.

[3]"To be master of oneself" *(jiyū, tzu-yu)* is not to be understood in the sense of will power or self-control. According to the biblical account, God created the world out of his free will: he was his own master, nobody compelled him; he was then a free, independent, autonomous guest. Each of us has something of this in him, the same in essence as the divine will.

[4]"Extraordinary" does not mean supernatural or miraculous. When true understanding is attained, the ordinaries transform themselves into extra-ordinaries.

[5]"Silent sage of the Śākya clan," an epithet of the Buddha.

[6]Buddhist psychology counts the intellect or consciousness *(manovijñāna)*, a discriminating agency, as the sixth sense. "The light emanating from the six senses" simply refers to their dynamic quality or readiness to respond.

[7]*Buji (wu-shih)* is one of the most significant terms in the vocabulary of Zen, especially in that of the Rinzai Sect. The term, however, is liable to be grossly misinterpreted by those who are not used to the Oriental way of living and feeling. It is a key term in the teaching of Rinzai.

When the Dharma is truly, fully, and existentially (experientially) understood, we find that there is nothing wanting in this life as we live it. Everything and anything we need is here with us and in us. One who has actually experienced this is called a man of *buji. Buji* is one of those concepts whose equivalents probably cannot be found in any European language, because in the thought-structure of the West there is nothing corresponding to it. "Non-action" or "not-doing" may do for Lao-tsu's *mu-i (wu-wei)*, and "no-mind" for Eno's *mushin (wu-hsin)*, but "no-business" or "no-event" sounds very queer for Rinzai's *buji*. The trouble with *buji* (or *muji*) is that there is no good word in English expressing all the ideas implied in *ji*.

*Ji (shih)* generally means "business," "event," "matter," "concern," "engagement," "affair," etc. When all this is negated, we may have for "a man of *buji*" "one who has no business," or "one to whom no events happen," or "one who is unconcerned or indifferent or disinterested," or "one to whom nothing matters," and so on. But "a man of *buji*" is not any of them. He is the one who has a true understanding of the Dharma or Reality as is described in the sermon; he has an existential insight into the Self; he is the one who being freed from externalities is master of himself; he is a Buddha and a patriarch. He has the great business of trying to lead all his fellow-beings into a state of enlightenment. He cannot remain unconcerned and indifferent so long as there is even one being left unemancipated. He works hard, "covered with ashes and smeared with mud," as Zen people would say; he is really one of the busiest men of the world, and yet he has "no business," "no events are happening to him," he is "utterly unconcerned." What kind of a man can he be? One of the "aristocracy," to use Eckhartian terminology; Zen calls him a "man of *buji*."

[8] *The Buddha is provided with a triple body (Trikāya): Dharmakāya,* the body of the Dharma; *Sambhogakāya,* the body of enjoyment; *Nirmāṇakāya,* the body of transformation. Rinzai's triple body has nothing to do with the Buddha's except in name. Rinzai thinks we can distinguish in our mind-activity these three aspects of the Buddha's Triple Body. The light of purity which is Aśvaghoṣa's *primary enlightenment* corresponds to the *Dharmakāya*. The light of non-discrimination may be regarded as the *Prajñā* (wisdom) aspect of the primary enlightenment, and the light of non-differentiation as the *Karuṇā* (compassion) aspect, whereby the *Dharmakāya* goes through all forms of transformation in order to deliver all beings from ignorance and its attendant fear and insecurity.

[9] Non-discrimination is intellectual, while non-differentiation is physical or objective. This is what I think Rinzai means.

[10] *Trikāya* in Sanskrit.

[11] The *sūtras* and *śāstras* are the canonical texts and philosophical treatises elucidating the teaching of the Buddha.

# *Love and Power*

A message read (in French and translated) by Dr. D. T. Suzuki in the Hall of the International Exhibition at Brussels on 28th May, 1958, at the Conference "In Defense of Spiritual Values in the Contemporary World."—ED.

Never in the history of mankind has there been a more urgent need for spiritual leaders and for the enhancement of spiritual values than there is in our contemporary world. We have achieved many wonderful things in this and the past century toward the advancement of human welfare. But, strangely, we seem to have forgotten that our welfare depends principally upon our spiritual wisdom and discipline. It is all due to our not fully recognizing this fact that we see the world at present being filled with the putrefying air of hatred and violence, fear and treachery. Indeed, we are trying to work all the harder for mutual destruction, not only individually but internationally and racially.

Of all the spiritual values we can conceive and wish to be brought out before us today, none is more commandingly needed than love.

It is love which creates life. Life cannot sustain itself without love. My firm conviction is that the present filthy, suffocating atmosphere of hatred and fear is generated through the suppression of the spirit of loving-kindness and universal brotherhood, and it goes without saying that this suffocation comes from the non-realization of the truth that the human community is the most complicated and far-reaching network of mutual dependence.

The moral teaching of individualism with all its significant corollaries is very fine indeed, but we must remember that the individual is non-existent when he is isolated from other individuals and cut off from the group to which he belongs, whether the group be biological or political or cosmological. Mathematically stated, the number one can never be one, never be itself, unless it is related to other numbers which are infinite. The existence of a single number by itself is unthinkable. Morally or spiritually, this means that the existence of each individual, whether or not he is conscious of the fact, owes something to an infinitely expanding and all-enwrapping net of loving relationship, which takes up not only every one of us but everything that exists. The world is a great family and we, each one of us, are its members.

I do not know how much geography has to do with the moulding of human thought, but the fact is that it was in the Far East that a system of thought developed in the seventh century which is known as the Kegon school of philosophy. The Kegan is based on the ideas of interfusion, or interpenetration, or interrelatedness, or mutual unobstructedness.

When this philosophy of the interrelatedness of things is rightly understood, love begins to be realized, because love is to recognize others and to take them into consideration in every way of life. To do to others what you would like them to do to you is the keynote of love and this is what naturally grows out of the realization of mutual relatedness.

The idea of mutual relationship and consideration excludes the notion of power, for power is something brought from outside into a structure of inner relationship. The use of power is always apt to be arbitrary and despotic and alienating.

What troubles us these days is no other than a crookedly exaggerated assertion of the power-concept by those who fail to see into its true nature and therefore are not capable of using it for the benefit of all.

Love is not a command given us by an outside agent, for this implies a sense of power. Excessive individualism is the hot-bed in which power-feeling is bred and nourished, because it is egocentric in the sense that it asserts itself arrogantly, and often violently, when it moves out of itself and tries to overrule others. Love, on the contrary, grows out of mutuality and interrelationship, and is far from egocentric and self-exalting. While power, superficially strong and irresistible, is in reality self-exhausting, love, through self-negation, is ever creative, for it is the root of existence. Love needs no external, all-powerful agent to exercise itself. Love is life and life is love.

Being an infinitely complicated network of interrelationship, life cannot be itself unless supported by love. Wishing to give life a form, love expresses itself in all modes of being. Form is necessarily individualistic, and the discriminating intellect is liable to regard form as final reality; the power-concept grows out of it. When the intellect develops and pursues its own course, being intoxicated by the success it has achieved in the utilitarian fields of human activity, power runs amok and plays havoc all around.

Love is affirmation, a creative affirmation; it is never destructive and annihilating, because unlike power it is all-embracing and all-forgiving. Love enters into its object and becomes one with it, while power, being characteristically dualistic and discriminative, crushes any object standing against it, or otherwise it conquers it and turns it into a slavish dependent.

Power makes use of science and everything that belongs to it. As long as science remains analytical and cannot go beyond the study of infinitely varied forms of differentiation and their quantitative measurements it is never creative. What is creative in it is its spirit of inquiry, which is inspired by love and not by power. Where there is any co-operation between power and the sciences, it always ends in contriving various methods of disaster and destruction.

Love and creativity are two aspects of one reality, but creativity is often separated from love. When this illegitimate separation takes place, creativity comes to be associated with power. Power really belongs to a lower order than love and creativity. When power usurps creativity, it becomes a most dangerous agent of all kinds of mischief.

The notion of power as aforesaid grows inevitably out of a dualistic interpretation of reality. When dualism neglects to recognize the presence of an integrating principle behind it, its native penchant for destruction exhibits itself rampantly and wantonly.

One of the most conspicuous examples of this display of power is seen in the Western attitude toward Nature. Westerners talk about conquering Nature and never about befriending her. They climb a high mountain and they declare the mountain is conquered. They succeed in shooting a certain type of projectile heavenwards and then claim that they have conquered the air. Why do they not say that they are now better acquainted with Nature? Unfortunately, the hostility-concept is penetrating every corner of the world and people talk about "control," "conquest," "conditioning," and the like.

The notion of power excludes the feelings of personality, mutuality, gratitude, and all kinds of relationship. Whatever benefits we may derive from the advancement of the sciences, ever-improving technology, and industrialization in general, we are not allowed to participate in them universally because power is liable to monopolize them instead of distributing them equally among our fellow beings.

Power is always arrogant, self-assertive, and exclusive, whereas love is self-humiliating and all-comprehensive. Power represents destruction, even self-destruction, quite contrary to love's creativeness. Love dies and lives again, while power kills and is killed.

It was Simone Weil, I understand, who defined power as a force which transforms a person into a thing. I would like to define love as a force that transforms a thing into a person. Love may thus appear to be something radically opposed to power, and love and power may be regarded as mutually exclusive, so that where there is power there cannot be any shadow of love, and where love is no power can ever intrude upon it.

This is true to a certain extent, but the real truth is that love is not opposed to power; love belongs to an order higher than power, and it is only power that imagines itself to be opposed to love. In truth, love is all-enveloping and all-forgiving; it is a universal solvent, an infinitely creative and resourceful agent. As power is always dualistic and therefore rigid, self-assertive, destructive, and annihilating, it turns against itself and destroys itself when it has nothing to conquer. This is in the nature of power, and is it not this that we are witnessing today, particularly in our international affairs?

What is blind is not love but power, for power utterly fails to see that its existence is dependent upon something else. It refuses to realize that it can be itself only allying itself to something infinitely greater than itself. Not knowing this fact, power plunges itself straight into the pit of self-destruction. The cataract that blinds the eye must be removed in order that power may experience enlightenment. Without this experience everything becomes unreal to the myopically veiled eye of power.

When the eye fails to see reality as it is, that is, in its suchness, a cloud of fear and suspicion spreads over all things that come before it. Not being able to see reality in its suchness, the eye deceives itself; it becomes suspicious of anything that confronts it and desires to destroy it. Mutual suspicion is thus let loose, and when this takes place no amount of explanation will reduce the tension. Each side resorts to all kinds of sophistry and subterfuge, which in international politics go under the name of diplomacy. But so long as there is nowhere any mutual trust and love, and the spirit of reconciliation, no diplomacy will alleviate the intensity of the situation which it has created by its own machinery.

Those who are power-intoxicated fail to see that power is blinding and keeps them within an ever-narrowing horizon. Power is thus associated with intellection, and makes use of it in every possible way. Love, however, transcends power because, in its penetration into the core of reality, far beyond the finiteness of the intellect, it is infinity itself. Without love one cannot see the infinitely expanding network of relationships which is reality. Or, we may reverse this and say that without the infinite network of reality we can never experience love in its true light. Love trusts, is always affirmative and all-embracing. Love is life and therefore creative. Everything it touches is enlivened and energized for new growth. When you love an animal, it grows more intelligent; when you love a plant you see into its every need. Love is never blind; it is the reservoir of infinite light.

Being blind and self-limiting, power cannot see reality in its suchness; and, therefore, what it sees is unreal. Power itself is unreal, and thus all that comes in contact with it turns into unreality. Power thrives only in a world of unrealities and thus it becomes the symbol of insincerity and falsehood.

To conclude: Let us first realize the fact that we thrive only when we are co-operative by being alive to the truth of interrelationship of all things in existence. Let us then die to the notion of power and conquest and be resurrected to the eternal creativity of love which is all-embracing and all-forgiving. As love flows out of rightly seeing reality as it is, it is also love that makes us feel that we—each of us individually and all of us collectively—are responsible for whatever things, good or evil, go on in our human community, and we must therefore strive to ameliorate or remove whatever conditions are inimical to the universal advancement of human welfare and wisdom.

# Buddhist Symbolism

Basho, one of the greatest *haiku*[1] poets in eighteenth century Japan, produced this when his eyes for the first time opened to the poetical and philosophical significance of *haiku*.

> *Furuike-ya!*
> *Kawazu tobi-komu*
> *Mizu-no oto!*

> Oh! ancient pond!
> A frog leaps in,
> The water's sound!

This is, as far as its literary sense goes, no more than the simple statement of the fact. Here is the ancient pond, probably partly covered with some aquatic plants and bordered with the bushes and weeds rampantly growing. The clear spring water, serenly undisturbed, reflects the trees with their fresh green foliage of the spring time, enhanced by a recent rainfall. A little green frog comes out of the grass and jumps into the water, giving rise to a series of ripples growing larger and larger until they touch the banks. The little frog jumping into the water should not make much of a sound. But when it takes place in a quiet environment it cannot pass unnoticed by Basho, who was in all likelihood absorbed in deep contemplation of nature. However feeble the sound might have been, it was enough to awaken him from his meditation. So he set down in the seventeen-syllable *haiku* what went through his consciousness.

Now the question is: What was this experience Basho, the poet, had at the moment?

As far as the *haiku* itself is concerned, it does not go beyond the matter of fact statement of the phenomenon of which he was the witness. There is no reference to what may be termed the subjective

[1] *Haiku* is the shortest form of poetic expression in Japanese literature.

aspect of the incident except the little particle, *ya*. Indeed, the presence of *ya* is the key-word to the whole composition. With this the *haiku* ceases to be an objective description of the frog jumping into the old pond and of the sound of the water caused thereby.

So long as the old pond remains a container of a certain volume of water quietly reflecting the things around it, there is no life in it. To assert itself as reality, a sound must come out of it; a frog jumps into it, the old pond then proves to be dynamic, to be full of vitality, to be of significance to us sentient beings. It becomes an object of interest, of value.

But there is one important observation we have to make, which is that the value of the old pond to Basho, the poet and seer (or mystic), did not come from any particular source outside the pond but from the pond itself. It may be better to say, the pond is the value. The pond did not become significant to Basho because of his finding the value in the pond's relationship to anything outside the pond as a pond.

To state this in other words, the frog's jumping into the pond, its causing the water to splash and make a noise, was the occasion—intellectually, dualistically, or objectively speaking—to make Basho realize that he was the pond and the pond was he, and that whatever value there was in this identification, the value was no other than the fact of this identification itself. There was nothing added to the fact.

When he recognized the fact, the fact itself became significant. Nothing was added to it. The pond was a pond, the frog was a frog, the water was water. The objects remained the same. No, it is better to express the idea in this way: no objective world, so called, at all existed with its frogs, ponds, etc., until one day a person known as Basho came suddenly to the scene and heard "the water's sound." The scene, indeed, until then had no existence. When its value was recognized by Basho this was to Basho the beginning or the creation of an objective world. Before this, the old pond was there as if it were not in existence. It was no more than a dream; it had no reality. It was the occasion of Basho's hearing the frog that the whole world, including the poet himself, sprung out of Nothingness *ex nihilo*.

There is still another way of describing Basho's experience and the birth of an objective world.

In their moment there was no participation, on the part of Basho, in the life of the old pond or of the little green frog. Both subject and object were totally annihilated. And yet the pond was the pond, Basho was Basho, the frog was the frog; they remained as they were, or as they have been from the beginningless past. And yet Basho was no other than the pond when he faced the pond; Basho was no other than the frog when he heard the sound of the water caused by its leaping. The leaping, the sound, the frog, and the pond, and Basho were all in one and one in all. There was an absolute totality, that is, an absolute identity, or, to use Buddhist terminology, a perfect state of Emptiness *(i.e., śūnyatā)* or Suchness *(i.e., tathatā).* Intellectualists or logicians may declare that all these different objects of nature are symbols, as far as Basho is concerned, of the highest value of reality. That this is not the view I have tried to explain is quite evident, I believe.

Why did Basho exclaim, *"Furuike-ya!"* "Oh! Old pond!"? What significance does this *"ya!",* corresponding to the English "Oh!" in this case, have to the rest of the *haiku*? The particle has the force of singling out the old pond from the rest of the objects or events and of making it the special point of reference. Thus, when the pond is mentioned, not only the series of events as particularly mentioned in the *haiku* but an infinite, inexhaustible totality of things making up the human world of existence comes along with it. The old pond of Basho is the *Dharma-dhātu* in the Kegon system of Buddhist philosophy. The old pond contains the whole cosmos and the whole cosmos finds itself securely held in the pond.

This idea may be illustrated by an infinite series of natural numbers. When we pick up any one of these numbers, for example, 5, we know that it is 1 (one) so many times repeated, that this repetition is not merely mechanical but organically related, and, therefore, that the series is an organic whole so closely and solidly united that when any one of the numbers is missing the whole series ceases to be a series (or group), and, further, that each unit thus represents or symbolizes the whole.

Take a number designated 5. 5 is not just 5. It is organically related to the rest of the series. 5 is 5 because of its being related to all the other numbers as units and also to the series as a whole. Without this 5 the whole is no more a whole, nor can all the other units (6, 4, 7, 8, 9, etc.) be considered belonging to the series. 5 then not only contains in it all the rest of the numbers in the infinite series, but it is also the series itself.

It is in this sense when the Buddhist philosophy states that all is one and one is all, or that the one is the many and the many the one.

Basho's *haiku* of "the old pond" now becomes perhaps more intelligible. The old pond with the frog jumping into it and producing a sound which not only spatially but temporally reaches the end of the world, is in the *haiku* by no means the ordinary pond we find everywhere in Japan, and the frog, too, is no common "green frog" of the spring time. To the author of the *haiku* "I" am the old pond, "I" am the frog, "I" am the sound, "I" am reality itself including all these separate individual units of existence. Basho at this moment of spiritual exaltation is the universe itself, nay, he is God Himself, Who uttered the fiat, "Let there be light." The fiat corresponds to "the sound of the water," for it is from this "sound" that the whole world takes its rise.

This being so, do we call "the old pond" or the water's sound or the leaping frog a symbol for the ultimate reality? In Buddhist philosophy there is nothing behind the old pond, because it is complete in itself and does not point to anything behind or beyond or outside itself. The old pond (or the water or the frog) itself is reality.

If the old pond is to be called a symbol because of its being an object of sense, intellectually speaking, then the frog is a symbol, the sound is a symbol, Basho is a symbol, the pen with which I write this is a symbol, the paper is a symbol, the writer is a symbol, indeed, the whole world is a symbol, including what we designate "reality." Symbolism may thus go on indefinitely.

Buddhist symbolism would therefore declare that everything is symbolic, it carries meaning with it, it has values of its own, it exists by its own right pointing to no reality other than itself. Fowls of the air and lilies of the field are the divine glory itself. They do not exist because of God. God Himself cannot exist without them, if God is assumed to be existing somewhere.

An old learned Chinese dignitary once said to a Zen master: "Chuang-tze announces that heaven and earth are one horse, the ten thousand things are one finger; is this not a wonderful remark?" The master without answering this pointed at a flower in the courtyard and said: "People of the world see the flower as if in a dream."

Zen Buddhism avoids generalization and abstraction. When we say that the whole world is one finger or that at the end of a hair Mount Sumeru dances, this is an abstraction. It is better to say with the ancient

Zen master that we fail to see the flower as it is, for our seeing is as if in a dream. We see the flower as a symbol and not as reality itself. To Buddhists, being is meaning. Being and meaning are one and not separable; the separation or bifurcation comes from intellection and intellection distorts the suchness of things.

There is another *haiku* giving the Buddhist idea of symbolization. This was composed by a woman poet of the nineteenth century. It runs like this:

> *Asagao-ya!*
> *Tsurube torarete*
> *Morai mizu.*

> Oh! the morning glory!
> The bucket seized away,
> I beg for water.

When the poet early in the morning went out to draw water from a well situated outdoors, she found the bucket entwined by a morning glory in bloom. She was so deeply impressed by the beauty of the flower that she forgot all about her mission. She just stood before it. When she recovered from the shock or trance, as it were, the only words she could utter were "Oh! The morning glory!" She did not describe the flower. She merely exclaimed as she did. No reference whatever to its beauty, to its ethereal beauty, did she make, showing how deeply, how thoroughly she was impressed by it. She was, in fact, carried away by it; she was the flower and the flower was she. They were so completely one that she lost her identity. It was only when she woke from the moment of unconscious identity that she realized that she was the flower itself or rather Beauty itself. If she were a poet standing before it and admiring its beauty, she would never have exclaimed, "Oh! The morning glory!" But as soon as she regained consciousness all that comes out of it inevitably followed, and she suddenly remembered that she was by the well because she wanted some water for her morning work. Hence the remaining two lines:

> The bucket seized away,
> I beg for water.

It may be noted that the poet did not try to undo the entwining vine. If she wanted to, this could have been easily done, for the morning glory yields readily to this process without being hurt. But evidently she had no desire to touch the flower with her earthly hands. She lovingly felt it as it was. She went to her neighbor to get the necessary water. She says the bucket was seized away by the flower. It is remarkable that she does not make any reference whatever to her defiling the transcendental beauty of the thing she sees before her. It was her womanly tenderness and passivity to refer to the captivity of the bucket.

Here again we see that there is no symbolism, for to the poet the morning glory does not symbolize beauty; it is beauty itself; it does not point to what is beautiful or of value; it is the value itself. There is no value to be sought outside the morning glory. Beauty is not something to be conceived beyond the flower. It is not a mere idea which is to be symbolized or concretized in the morning glory. The morning glory is the whole thing. It is not that the poet comes to beauty through or by means of what our senses and intellect distinguish as individual objects. The poet knows no other beauty than the morning glory as she stands beside it. The flower is beauty itself: the poet is beauty itself. Beauty recognizes beauty, beauty finds itself in beauty. It is because of human senses and intellect that we have to bifurcate beauty and talk about one who sees a beautiful object. As long as we cling to this way of thinking, there is symbolism. But Buddhist philosophy demands not to be blindfolded by so-called sense objects, for they will forever keep us away from reality itself.

We see, therefore, that there is something corresponding in Buddhism to what is ordinarily known as symbolism. Buddhism is, so to speak, thoroughly realistic in the sense that it does symbolize any particular object in distinction to something else. Buddhists would assert that if there is anything at all to be distinguished as a symbol bearing a specific value, the value here referred to has no realistic sense whatever. For there can be no such object to be specifically distinguishable. If anything is a symbol, everything is also equally a symbol, thus putting a stop to symbolism.

Symbolism in Buddhist philosophy may be said to be of a different connotation from what philosophers generally understand by the term.

# Ignorance and
# World Fellowship

## 1

According to the basic teaching of Buddhism which is accepted by all
Buddhists, Hīnayāna and Mahāyāna, it is from Ignorance that there is
Karma. In the Twelvefold Chain of Origination, we have *Saṃskāra*
instead of Karma; but both terms are derived from the same root *kṛi,*
which means "to do," "to act," or "to work," and practically they are
equivalent to the English word, "action." To state that Action starts
from Ignorance, or that, dependent on Ignorance there is Action,
means that the world where we live and carry on our business is the
product of Ignorance. For the world is our Karma, or the world is the
stage for Karma to work out its destiny.

Ignorance is an epistemological term and Karma has a moral signification. They appear to belong to different spheres of thought, and we
may well ask how it is possible for the one to issue from the other. In
Buddhism, however, Ignorance has a more fundamental connotation,
and points to the awakening of the intellect itself. This awakening is an
act, and we can state that Ignorance is Karma and Karma is Ignorance;
it is not, strictly speaking, quite right to establish a causal relation
between the two terms, they are simply two aspects of the same fact. But
because of the general intellectual tendency of Buddhism, Ignorance is
mentioned first and spoken of as if Karma stands to it in the relation of
dependence. In our practical life wherever there is Karma there is
Ignorance and wherever there is Ignorance there is Karma. The two
cannot be separated. To understand what they exactly mean is to have
an insight into the Buddhist conception of the world and life. The aim
of the Buddhist discipline is to overcome Ignorance, which is also
freeing oneself from Karma, and all its consequences.

What, then, does it mean when we say that "the world is Ignorance and Karma"? It means that the world starts from discrimination, for discrimination is Ignorance and the beginning of dualism—dualism of all kinds. Before discrimination started there was no Ignorance, but as soon as we began to discriminate between that which knows and that which is known, between *noesis* and *noema,* the shadow of Ignorance fell over the entire field of knowledge—knowledge is always now accompanied by ignorance. Since that time, we have been deeply engrossed with dualism itself, and fail to become conscious of that which underlies it. Most people think that dualism is final, that the subject for its own reason ever stands contrasted to the object, and *vice versa,* that there is no mediating bridge which crosses over the chasm between the two opposing concepts, and that this world of opposites remains forever as such, that is, in a state of eternal fighting. But this way of thinking is not quite right and logical according to Buddhist philosophy; for the absolute antithesis in which "A" stands against "not-A" is only possible when there is a third concept, as it were bridging the two terms. When this third concept is not recognized, there is Ignorance. And we must remember that this recognition is more than merely epistemological.

Non-discrimination underlies the discrimination of an antithesis. So long as this non-discrimination is not intuited, Ignorance remains undispelled, and casts its dark shadow over life. To be shut up in the clouds of Ignorance means the acceptance of Karma as the supremely dominant power of life. We are then overawed by Karma; we subject ourselves to the dominance of matter; we are no more a free-willing and self-acting agent, but part of a grand machine of whose inner mechanism we are entirely ignorant; we move as the dead leaves are swept about by the autumn wind.

But how is it possible to rise above Ignorance, to free ourselves from Karma which is matter, and to have a glimpse into the realm of non-discrimination? The possibility of achieving this will mean the doing away with the world, which is tantamount to committing suicide. If Ignorance can be transcended only by death, what is the use, one may ask, of transcending it? Let us remain ignorant and continue suffering—this is probably then our conclusion. But in this conclusion there is no consolation, no happiness, only a despair of the deepest nature; and this was exactly what we desired to conquer at the beginning.

2

The world in which we find ourselves existing is, as I said before, the outcome of Ignorance, that is, of discrimination, and because of this, there is Karma. For Karma is possible only when there is the duality of subject and object in their mutual relationship, and this subject must be a conscious one, conscious of what it is doing. If it were unconscious, there would be no Karma, and therefore no world such as we live in. The mountains may be found towering towards the sky, the oceans filled with waves, the wind blowing over the trees, and the birds chirping in the early spring morning. With all these multiple phenomena, the world is not our own world; it may be the one for rocks, waters, trees, animals, and also perhaps for divine beings, but most assuredly not for us human beings. There are enough movements, of all kinds, indeed, but not such as are known as Karma, that is, those with moral and religious significance.

While consciousness was not yet awakened, the world had no meaning; there were no values in it intellectual, moral, and aesthetic, in short, there was no Karma. With the rise of consciousness, there is discrimination, and with discrimination Ignorance creeps along; for discrimination is double-edged, the one side of which cuts well whereas the other side is altogether dull. It is like a mirror; its bright surface reflects everything which comes before it, but the reverse side of it has no light whatever. It is again like the sun: where it is most brilliantly illuminating, its shadow falls the deepest. The appearance of consciousness in the world means the creation of an objective environment standing against and working upon a subjective mind. Superficially, everything is now well-defined and clarified, but there always hovers a dark cloud of Ignorance over the horizon of consciousness. As long as this cloud is not somehow swept away, Karma assumes a threatening aspect, and there is no peace of mind with us. We must somehow be enlightened thoroughly, and the overshadowing Karma must be understood and thereby overcome.

But is this possible? Does not enlightenment mean the negation of the world? Is not death the outcome of the whole procedure? Are not death and *Nirvāṇa* synonymous?

3

In short, there are two ways of dispelling Ignorance and attaining Enlightenment. The one is negative and the other positive. The negative way is to deny the world, to escape it, to realise Arhatship, to enter into *Nirvāṇa,* to dream of Heaven, to be reborn into the Western Land of Bliss. The positive way is to assert the world, to fight it, to be mixed in it, to go through birth and death, to struggle with tribulations of all kinds, not to flinch in the face of threats and horrors. The first way has been resorted to by most religionists and the second by people of the world— men of action; that is, by business men and statesmen and soldiers. But the latter classes of people are most deeply involved in Ignorance, in the assertion of egotistic passions, and far from being enlightened as to the meaning of life. The fact is not however to be denied that among them there have been quite a few who were really enlightened, masters of themselves as well as of the world.

The negative way is comparatively easier, but there is something about it not quite logical and it is inconsistent and antisocial. If the world is the outcome of discrimination and discrimination leads to Enlightenment, which is the dispelling of Ignorance, the world with all its evils—in whatever sense the term may be understood—must be accepted. If this is not done, we are led to dream of a Heaven where a state of absolute uniformity and mere inactivity prevails. Paradise is the death of all that makes up this world. There cannot be any community life in it, for there is no conflict in Heaven, and conflict is needed for a conscious being to have any feeling of himself and of beings other than himself. As long as discrimination is at the basis of our conscious life, we cannot consistently fly away from the world.

For this reason, the conception of an eternal life in the sense of a life beyond birth and death is untenable. Life means the struggle of birth and death. There can be no life where there is no death. Immortality is not a logical concept. It is no more than a dream. Life is a cloth woven of birth and death. The moment we are born, we are destined to die, in fact every moment means a constant succession of birth and death, of death and birth. To seek Enlightenment by negating the world, a world of birth and death, is really a deception. The negative way is not after all the solution of life.

The Buddhist way of solving the problem of life is a positive one. Buddhism accepts life as it is, faces its dualism, its evils, its struggles, its pains, in fact everything that makes it up. Life is Karma which is the outcome of discrimination; and there is no escaping this Karma inasmuch as discrimination is at the basis of all that makes up the world and life. To escape it is to commit suicide, but suicide is also a Karma and bears its fruit and the suicide is born again to a life of pain and suffering.

Enlightenment must come from truly recognizing the meaning of birth and death, and thereby transcending their dualism. Ignorance consists in regarding dualism as final and clinging to it as the basis of our communal life. This logically and emotionally ends in egotism and all the evils flowing from its assertion. Buddhism asks us to gain an insight into that which underlies all forms of dualism and thereby not to be attached to them as irreducively final.

## 4

What is this "that which underlies" the one and the many, birth and death, you and me, that which is and that which is not? It is not quite right to say "underlies," for it suggests the opposition between that which lies under and that which lies over—which is a new dualism; and when we go on like this, we commit the fault of infinite regression. According to Buddhism, this third term is designated *śūnyatā,* Emptiness. All opposites rise from it, sink into it, exist in it.

*Śūnyatā* is apt to be misunderstood by all of us whose so-called logical mind fails to conceive anything going beyond relativity. *Śūnyatā* is set against reality and understood as non-reality or nothingness or void. I generally translate it Emptiness.

*Śūnyatā* is not the Absolute as it is usually understood, when the Absolute is regarded as a something standing by itself. Such an Absolute is really non-existent, for there is nothing in this world which is absolutely separable from the rest of it. If there is such a one existent, we have nothing to do with it.

*Śūnyatā* is not God, for *śūnyatā* is not personal, nor is it impersonal. If it is at all personal, its personality must be infinitely different from what we generally conceive of personality. As long as human beings rise from *śūnyatā*, the latter must be regarded as to that extent personal and self-conscious. But it would be a grave error to try to find any parallelism between human personality and that of *śūnyatā*.

Nor is *śūnyatā* to be conceived atheistically, nor pantheistically, nor acosmistically. Therefore, Buddhism which upholds the idea of *śūnyatā* is not a godless religion, nor is it pantheistic as it is sometimes most incorrectly conceived. Nor is it acosmism.

*Śūnyatā* is sometimes identified with the Universal which is really non-existent. Devoid of all contents, the Universal is a mere logical concept and cannot be operative in this world of particulars.

5

The relation of *śūnyatā* to the dualism of existence will be illustrated by the following two Zen *mondōs*.

A monk came to Tōzan (T'ung-shan, 807–869) and asked: "Cold and heat alternately come and go, and how can one escape them?" The question has the same purport as this, "How can one transcend the dualism of birth and death, of being and non-being?" The Christian way of putting it may be, "How can one attain an immortal life?" As Zen does not follow an abstract, conceptualistic method of teaching, it is always in touch with the concrete facts of life.

The master answered: "Why not go where there is neither cold nor heat?" This may suggest the idea that Buddhism advocates the running away from the world, or its negation. Apparently, it does, if we do not go any farther than the bare statement by the master. But listen to what follows. The monk asked, "Where is the place where there is neither cold nor heat?" The questioner evidently took the master's answer for what we would generally do, i.e., a realm of absolute transcendence. The master however said, "When the cold season is here, we all feel cold; when the hot season arrives, we also all feel warm." This is where neither cold nor heat troubles us.

The actual outcome of Tōzan's answer is that where you suffer cold or heat is where there is neither cold nor heat. This is a paradoxical saying, but the ultimate truth of all religion is paradoxical, and there is no way to avoid it as long as we are sticklers to formal logic. To translate the idea in terms of regular Buddhist terminology, *śūnyatā* is to be found at the very seat of birth and death, or, more directly, *śūnyatā* is birth and death, and birth and death is *śūnyatā*. Yet they are not identical. *Śūnyatā* is *śūnyatā*, birth-and-death is birth-and-death. They are distinct, and are to be kept distinct when we desire to have a clear grasp of the fact itself.

A similar question was asked of Sōzan (T'sang-shan, 840–901), disciple of Tōzan: "The hot season is at its height, and how shall we escape it?" The experience of pain is universal, and all religion starts from pessimism, for without the experience of pain in one form or another there will be no reflection on life and without reflection no religion. Sōzan's answer was: "Escape into the midst of the seething waters, into the midst of a blazing coal." The Zen master's advice is like pouring oil into a fire; instead of being an escape in the ordinary sense of the word, it is aggravating pain, bringing it to its acutest point; and when there is thus no soothing of pain, where is the escape we are so earnestly in search of?

The monk has not stopped here, and, wanting to pursue the matter to its ultimate end, asks, "How shall we escape the seething waters and the blazing coal?" The point may be somewhat difficult to comprehend, but it means this. When life is accepted, with all its pains and evils, where is our salvation? Heaven has been created for this purpose, and if we go to Hell as advised by Sōzan, what is the use of our at all trying to escape, to save ourselves? Hence the monk's second question. The master's answer was, "No further pains will harass you."

When thought is divided dualistically, it seeks to favor the one at the cost of the other, but as dualism is the very condition of thought, it is impossible for thought to rise above its own condition. The only way to do this is to accept dualism squarely, and not think of it any further. When you are to suffer a pain for one reason or another, you just suffer it, and have no other thoughts about it. When you are to enjoy a pleasure you just enjoy it, and have no other thoughts about it. By thus experiencing what comes to you, you experience *śūnyatā* in which there is neither dualism nor monism nor transcendentalism. This is what is meant by the statement which makes up the basic teaching of the *Prajñāpāramitā,* that "when I thus talk to you, there is no talk, nor any hearing; nor is there any talker, and no audience either"—which is *śūnyatā.*

This conception of *śūnyatā* in relation to a dualistic or pluralistic world is expressed in Buddhist philosophy by the formula: *Byōdō in shabetsu* and *shabetsu in byōdō*. *Byōdō* literally means "evenness and equality" and *shabetsu* "difference and division." *Byōdō* is sometimes taken to mean identity, or sameness, or the universal, and *shabetsu* individuality, or particularity, or multiplicity. But it is more correct to consider *byōdō* = *śūnyatā* = "that which lies underneath pluralistic existences," or "that from which individuals rise and into which individuals sink." Individuals always remain individuals in a dualistically-conditioned world; they are not the same in the sense that you are I and I am you, for you and I are antithetical and their merging into each other is the end of the world. But this does not mean that there is no bridging between the two terms, for if there were no bridging, there would be no mutuality, and consequently no communal life. This discrete and yet continuous state of existence is described by Buddhist philosophers as *"Byōdō in shabetsu* and *shabetsu in byōdō."* Or, for brevity's sake, *"Byōdō soku shabetsu* and *shabetsu soku byōdō." Soku* is a copulative particle expressing equation or identity.

6

This being so, Buddhists frankly accept this world of pluralities with all its moral and intellectual complexities. They advise us not to try to escape it, because after all no escape is possible, wherever you go your shadow follows you. A monk asked a master, "How is it possible to escape the triple world?" Answered the master, "What is the use of escaping it?" The triple world of desire, of form, and of no-form is the place where we have our being and live our lives; our trying to escape it in order to find a land of bliss somewhere else is like a lunatic seeking his own head which he never lost. When the founder of the Myōshinji monastery was requested by a monk to help him get out of the cycle of birth and death, the founder roared, "Here in my place there is no birth-and-death." This answer in its final purport is not at all negativistic, it ultimately points to the same idea as given vent to by the other masters.

With consciousness once awakened, discrimination inevitably follows its steps, and on the reverse side of discrimination Ignorance is found. Ignorance shades our life as long as it is the ruling principle of the world, as long as we are unable to see behind a world of dualities and hence of pluralities. In short, if we hold up this dualistically-conditioned existence as finality, and altogether leave out the mediating notion of *śūnyatā* from which individual things rise and to which they return, and by which they are interrelated one to another while in existence, then we become incurably either crass materialists or dreamy idealists. Ignorance is dispelled only when we have an insight into *śūnyatā*.

Enlightenment may sound more or less intellectual, but in point of fact it illuminates life itself and all that makes up life is cleansed of its taints. Love now shines in its true life. Although differences are recognized and accepted, they cease to be the condition of antagonistic feelings—which latter is usually the case with us enlightened. Fellowship becomes an actuality. Here is the ideal of Bodhisattvahood.

Arhatship, which has been upheld by Buddhists as the supreme type of mankind, is not unconditionally countenanced by followers of Mahāyāna Buddhism. The latter recognize the dominating power played by the material world over the welfare for all beings, they endeavour to save them from all forms of misery, material and spiritual, and they are even willing to sacrifice their own welfare for others. In order to carry out their altruistic impulses, they are ever resourceful, they devise every possible means to attain the end they have in view— the work of universal salvation.

7

In the *Kwannon Sūtra,* Kwannon is made to incarnate himself in thirty-three different forms in order to realize his inexhaustible love-feeling toward all beings. According to Mahāyāna Buddhism, all enlightened ones are Kwannons and are able to manifest themselves in an infinite number of bodies when necessary. Kwannon is sometimes represented with eleven heads and one thousand hands. Eleven is ten plus one, symbolizing infinity, for Kwannon is infinitely capable of looking around and picking up those requiring his help; and one thousand arms mean Kwannon's utmost resourcefulness to carry out his mission of love.

It may not be out of place to refer in this connection to some aspects of Kwannon's, or any Bodhisattva's, love-activity. Love with him does not always mean mere apparent friendliness, for it may frequently take a form of hatred or any adverse feeling. Conditions in which the subject concerned may find himself may be externally unfavorable ones, at least humanly judging. They may even be to all appearances highly threatening and destructive. The Bodhisattva may sometimes appear to him in the form of an inanimate object—a piece of rock, a block of wood, etc., which, in a most mysterious way, afford him an opportunity to see into the secret sources of reality.

8

One of the greatest things religion has neglected in the past is the material aspect of life. Religion has emphasized too much its spiritual side, while spirit and matter are so intimately related that the one cannot go without the other. Since the rise of science, followed by the initiation of the machine age and capitalism, matter has come to assert itself at the expense of spirit, and religion which has been such a strong friend of the latter is at present steadily losing her power over mankind. In the face of modern armed nations ready to fall at one another's throat, religion is entirely helpless. Spiritual fellowship is closely related to material fellowship—we must not forget this fact.

It is in matter as well as in spirit that we feel fellowship and mutuality. Spirit often tends towards individualism, and matter towards communism. Matter is a world common to us all, for it is over matter that we exercise our spiritual power and feel our own existence. Matter resists our approach, and by this we grow conscious of ourselves, that is, of our own spirituality. In this respect, matter is our friend, not our enemy. Whatever resistance it may offer, it is to help us grow stronger in our spiritual power. When matter is attacked with any antagonistic feeling, the feeling reacts on us, and instead of really strengthening the spirit, sours its temper, and hatred is lodged in it.

Matter has hitherto been kept down too despisingly and it is revenging itself now upon the spirit—this is one way of explaining the present state of unrest all over the world. Matter has the just claim to be treated in a more friendly spirit.

From the Buddhist point of view, it is not right to keep matter from spirit and spirit from matter separated as fundamentally irreducible to each other. It is due to our intellectual discrimination that we have come to espouse dualism and hence the antagonism of matter and spirit. Ever since this separation, which is the outcome of Ignorance, the world knows no rest, no peace. As far as the Buddhist teaching is concerned, however, it stops with the wiping out of this Ignorance.

As to the management of the so-called material world, together with our communal life, national and international, which is based on matter, it is left to the best judgments of "worldly" wise people. The only direction Buddhism can given them is to remind them of the truth that as long as Ignorance, taken in its widest possible sense, has a firm hold of us, we are never able to rise above its most undesirable and most deplorable consequences. All these consequences are in fact the outcome of "love" wrongly directed by Ignorance. The removal of Ignorance has really far-reaching effects on human society.

## 9

Love *(karuṇā)* is the moving principle of all forms of fellowship. When this is misdirected, egotism results in every possible manner—individual egotism, national egotism, racial egotism, economic egotism, religious egotism, and so on. We are suffering at present most poignantly from all these various forms of egotism. Religion, which is supposed to combat the centripetal tendencies of egotism, is to all appearances entirely powerless to cope with the present situation.

Religion is never tired of teaching us to get rid of selfishness, but when the question concerns international or interracial or other world affairs, the teaching has no practical effects upon us. A corporation is noted for its being free from conscience, so is a nation. Legal subterfuges are liberally resorted to, to gain the object of its selfishness. Patriotism, or corporation spirit, differs from personal egotism in that the former is a congregation of individuals who are united with a common purpose. When it sustains a loss in one form or another, usually along the line of economy and political prestige, the loss is shared by the whole body. The directors feel, therefore, responsible for all their doings and also cherish a moral sense of public-spiritedness.

Public-spiritedness is all very well as far as it goes, but when it implies egotism of a fierce kind, and tends to exclusiveness at all costs, we know where it finally ends. We are just witnessing it practically demonstrated all over the world. And the saddest thing of all is that we are helpless to check its reckless progress towards an inevitable end. We have, perhaps, to submit to the logical working of our own Karma, which we have been accumulating since the beginningless past.

How can we rise from this almost hopeless state of affairs which we witness today everywhere about us? The easiest way is for us to become at once conscious of our own Ignorance and thereby to break off the fetters of Karma. But this is what is the most difficult task in the world to accomplish; we have been trying to do this all our lives throughout innumerable ages of the past.

If it is impossible for us, advocating the various faiths of the world, to stem the tide even when we know where it is finally tending, the only thing we can do is to preserve a little corner somewhere on earth, East or West, where our faiths can be safely guarded from utter destruction. When all the turmoils are over, if possible with the least amount of damage, material and otherwise, we may begin to think seriously of the folly we have so senselessly been given up to, and seek the little corner we have saved for this purpose.

If this sounds too negative, let all the large-hearted Bodhisattvas in the world get together and use their moral influence to the utmost of their abilities, and keep their spiritual fire, however solitary it may be, burning at its intensest. From the Buddhist point of view the main thing is to become enlightened regarding the signification of Ignorance and Karma, which, not being fully comprehended, darkens the purport of world-fellowship.

10

Let me suggest some practical methods of leading to Enlightenment, as proposed by all Buddhism. For individual Enlightenment, the six virtues of *Pāramitā* are recommended: Charity, Morality, Humility, Virility (or Indefatigability), Meditation, and Wisdom (or Transcendental Knowledge). In some schools of Buddhism, the last two *Pāramitās* are specially emphasized, but we must remember that Meditation and Wisdom have some well-defined connotation in Buddhism.

When individuals are enlightened, we are apt to think that the whole world too will attain Enlightenment, which means a millennium. But the fact is that universal Enlightenment is not the sum-total of individual Enlightenments, for individuals are always found connected, on account of Karma, which is to say, of history, with different communal groups such as races, nations, castes, etc. To rise above these Karma-hindrances it is necessary, at least as one of the practical methods of achieving the end—the world-fellowship of faiths—to have free communication of all kinds among religiously-aspiring people of different nations. This means free travelling—the establishment of various learned institutes for the understanding of different religions, or different cultures, the exchange of religious representatives corresponding to the exchange of ambassadors among nations, the summoning of a religious parliament which will consider various means of attaining world peace, etc., etc.

That at present no nations are willing to have a world religious conference, somewhat reminding us of a naval disarmament conference or of a league of nations, positively demonstrates the truth that our Karma-hindrance still weighs on us too heavily, and probably we have to wait patiently for our Karma to work itself out, although this does not imply that some enlightened individuals endeavour to work for universal Enlightenment in the best ways they can conceive and according to their vows, i.e., *praṇidhāna*.

# *Explaining Zen I*

My way of explaining Zen may not be altogether the traditional way, but according to my understanding, the origin of Zen is traceable to Buddha's experience of Enlightenment about twenty-five hundred years ago in the northern part of India. Buddhism developed out of the Buddha's experience, and this experience is known as Enlightenment. In Sanskrit it is called *Bodhi,* and *Bodhi* and *Buddha* both come from the same root *budh. Bodhi* means Enlightenment and Buddha means the Enlightened One, so when we talk about Buddhism or Buddha, we have to connect what we are saying with the Enlightenment experience of the Buddha. Without Enlightenment Buddhism would have no meaning whatever, and when Zen claims to transmit the essential experience of Buddha we have to go up to the plane of that Enlightenment. When this is understood Zen will be understood.

To be a good Zen Buddhist it is not enough to follow the teaching of its founder; we have to experience the Buddha's experience. When we just follow the teaching, that teaching, however noble and exalted it may be, does not become our own. Buddha did not want his followers to follow his teachings blindly. He wanted his disciples to experience what he himself experienced, and to have his teachings proved by each follower's personal experience. Experience, therefore, counts much more in Buddhism than its teaching. In other religions the founder expects his teachings to be followed by his devotees, who do not necessarily repeat the experience of the founder. The founder gives instructions, and the followers follow those instructions; they do not necessarily experience the same experience. In some religions the repetition of such experience is even considered to be impossible because the founder's experience is divine, and we humans cannot have the same divine experience.

Buddhism, on the other hand, declares that so long as we can talk about the divine nature, whatever it may be, to that extent the divine nature must be our own. If it is our own, there is no reason why it cannot be experienced, and revealed within ourselves. This may be thought an ambitious aspiration. But to call it ambition is already degrading ourselves. Rather is it a most righteous aspiration, for all human aspirations come out of this divine nature. It is therefore natural for us all to reveal that divine nature in ourselves, instead of leaving it as something unexperienced.

Zen, therefore, aims to come in contact with that divine nature which is in us all, and this revelation of the divine nature in ourselves is what constitutes the Enlightenment experience of Buddha. This divine nature is what we may call the Absolute Self. When we talk about self it is generally confused with relative self, which is to be distinguised from the Absolute Self. When this distinction is not clearly made we are apt to take the individual, empirical, psychological self as the divine nature or Absolute Self. When we say "I am," this "I" is generally considered to originate from a relative "I." But the relative "I" cannot stand by itself; it must have something *behind* it which makes "I" possible, which makes this "I" really "I" in its deepest possible sense. If there is no real Absolute Self behind this relative, psychological "I," this psychological "I" will never achieve its I-ness. The relative "I" assumes something of the real "I" because it has at its back the real "I." When this "Absolute I" is taken away no relative "I" exists. But in our ordinary way of thinking this relative "I" is separated from "Absolute I," and we take this separated "I" as something absolute—something independent, something that can stand on its own right. When this notion is adhered to we have what we call egotism, the ego-centered notion which ordinarily governs our consciousness.

Now Buddhism talks about the *ātman* and *Non-ātman,* and Buddha taught the doctrine of *Non-ātman,* that is, the No-ego doctrine.

There is no ego, there is no *ātman.* When this kind of teaching is understood more or less superficially people judge Buddhism as something negative, or annihilistic. But, as we all know, nothing can stand on a negation. Negation can never stand by itself; it always implies something positive, something affirmative. The reason I can say "I am" is because this "I" stands on a great affirmation. "I am" is affirmation, and when this affirmation is understood in its positive sense we have the Enlightenment experience. When Buddhism denies the *ātman* this *ātman* is not Absolute *Ātman* but relative *ātman.* When this relative *ātman* is negated, the very negation implies that there is something affirmative behind it, and this affirmation is nothing but Absolute Self. Enlightenment brings out this Absolute Self in its original "Suchness." Buddhism, therefore, ought not to be understood in a negative sense.

In the same way, when Zen developed in China it took up the doctrine advanced by Nāgārjuna, the great Indian philosopher, who lived soon after the birth of Christ. His doctrine is based on the *Prajñā-pāramitā Sūtra,* which contains a famous series of negations in which everything is denied. This is quite natural, because our ordinary way of thinking is characterized by relativity, by bifurcation, dichotomy, the separation of subject and object. But this Enlightenment experience, the revelation of the Absolute Self, is beyond this dualistic way of thinking. We therefore naturally start by negating all those forms of dichotomy. But if we start with a negation, one negation not being enough, we go on negating continuously. This series of negations can never come to any conclusion; but when we realize that each negation implies in it an affirmation there is no need to repeat negations; one negation is enough.

A Zen Teacher in China used to hold up the stick which he carried, and say "If you call this stick a stick you touch," that is, you affirm. "When you do not call this stick a stick you turn against," that is, you negate. "So this stick—you cannot call it a stick, nor can you call it not a stick. So neither affirmation nor negation will do. Without negating, without asserting, make a statement!"

Zen teachers demonstrate ordinary every day truth in the same familiar way—by taking up a knife or fork, or picking up a book, or producing a hand with just one finger sticking up. "If you say this is a finger, that is assertion. If you do not call it a finger, that is negation. Then what do you call it?" Finger or hand or fist or stick, it does not make any difference. Whenever you say something it is either a negation or an affirmation. Apart from those two, we cannot say anything. But the teacher demands that you say something about it. What will you say?

One way of answering that kind of problem is recorded in a Zen book. A monk came out of the congregation, took the stick away from the master, broke it into two pieces and threw them away. But if we do the same as that monk did there is no Zen. That would be simply an imitation. Each individual must have his or her own original way of solving the problem. Someone may say, it is a stick just the same. Another may say it is not a stick. Whatever you say, that will also do; it all depends what inner experience you have had. Out of that experience assertion may come or negation may come or breaking the stick into several pieces—that may also come. Or you may ask the teacher: "What do *you* call the stick?" That will also do. All kinds of answers are possible, but if you imitate somebody else there will be no Zen. An individual original experience is needed, but backed by that experience you can swing the stick in any way you like. Otherwise your answers will be just dead things; there will be no life in them.

So this Absolute Self, unless it is most intimately, innerly experienced, will, when we say "I am that I am," be nonsense. When God appeared on Mount Sinai and pronounced his name to Moses as "I am that I am" he was right; for that was God's name. It was God himself. If we can really say "I am that I am," as Christ said, "I am before Abraham was," there is Absolute Self revealed. But this revelation is not just talking about it; it must be a real personal experience.

When the Buddha began to search for Self he wanted to find Self. What made him go through the cycle of birth and death? He wanted to know. When he knew what he was, he could really transcend this eternal cycle of birth and death, this flux of becoming. In modern terms we talk much about a stream or flux of becoming, but the Buddha's problem was to cross over this stream of becoming, to emerge out of becoming and see something in becoming itself. To do this he had first to divide himself. He had to analyze what his self was, to project a question out of himself. The analysis consisted in dividing himself, which is, from the ordinary point of view, impossible. To see what his self was, he projected himself as a second self and began to dissect that second self, to see what real Self was. That is an impossible task, but we all do that when we intellectualize—when we appeal to intellection. When he proposed a question, that was going out of himself. He projected himself as not-self, because the question went out of himself and he wanted by questioning to dissect himself. He could not apply his knife of dissection on himself. Intellectually he had to put himself out, that is, to negate himself. But this negation was killing himself. However precise, however logical that dissection may be, it is not he himself, but something projected out of himself. That is his second self, not the real Self. So however much he may analyze, he can never get at the real

Self, because real Self is himself. So it is altogether impossible, we might say, to dissect himself. To dissect himself is murdering himself. When he himself is murdered, nothing is left. The analyst himself and the subject he tries to analyze both disappear. Therefore, to understand what the Self is we must go back within the Self instead of having that self projected out of real Self—we must go back. Instead of intellectually trying to locate that self we must go deep within ourselves and take hold of it. That is impossible, but that is what we must all try to do, and unless we succeed we can never be rescued. And the Buddha succeeded.

The proof that he succeeded in taking hold of his Absolute Self does not come from the Buddha himself but comes out of ourselves. If the Buddha tried to prove his realization, that proof would naturally appeal to words, or to some kind of gesture. When it is expressed that way the expression is not the real one, but is only real in reference to the Buddha himself. When we try to take that reference, and to go back to its origin—Buddha himself—that can only be done by ourselves experiencing it. As long as we take up his intellectual reference as something real, that is taking the finger which points at the moon for the moon itself. When the moon is seen there is no need for the finger. The moon must be seen though the finger is needed to point at the moon. So long as the moon is not seen the finger is nothing but a finger. So with the Buddha's experience, we know that the Buddha's experience is true when we know it from our own experience.

A certain kind of reasoning used by an ancient master is recorded in one of the Zen books, and it reads like this:

Someone asked the master; "What is meant by seeing into the nature?" This nature means Buddha-nature, and everything is in possession of Buddha-nature, which is Absolute Self. So the monk's question is: What is the Absolute Self? What is the Self that makes us really say: "I am," that makes God say: "I am that I am"? This question, therefore, is most fundamental, for when we get into this nature we attain Buddhahood, we experience Enlightenment. And Zen starts from this. Therefore this question is the most fundamental one.

The master said: "The Buddha-nature (or Absolute Self) in its purity remains serene from the first and shows no movement whatever. It is free of all categories such as being and non-being, long and short, grasping and giving up, purity and defilement. It stands by itself in tranquility." Note that the Buddhist sense of purity is metaphysical, not merely ethical. Nature in its absoluteness remains serene, and serene means free from becoming. "And shows no movement whatever" means that there is no becoming when the nature remains in its absoluteness. This corresponds to the Western conception of Godhead. The Godhead remains serene, pure, unmoved and unmoving. It is not a creator; it is not created. Godhead exactly corresponds to this Buddha-nature, as explained by this Zen teacher.

All categories such as being and non-being, pure, defiled, long, and short, belong to this world. The world of relativity uses such standards of measurement, but these standards do not apply to the nature itself. To describe this state of being Buddhists say it is in tranquility, in this absolute state of tranquility. And where this nature is seen, it is called "seeing the nature." This nature is Buddha himself, and his Enlightenment. So to see the nature will be to see Buddha, to attain Enlightenment, to become cognizant of Absolute Self.

Now the question arises: when the nature is already pure, and does not belong to such categories as being and non-being, how can there be any seeing? When we talk about seeing, seeing implies one who sees and that which is seen. If nature is so pure and so absolute that there is no division of subject and object, how *could* there be any seeing? That is quite a natural question and the master's answer is: "In seeing there is nothing seen." We say that we see but there is nothing seen. Really, seeing is no seeing. When the stick is produced and we say it is a stick, it is not a stick. When we say it is not a stick, the stick remains just the same. This is what the master means. But this is hard to see unless one goes through a certain experience, unless one has a certain form of intuition. Now the question is: if there is nothing seen, how can one speak of seeing at all? This is also a natural question. The master replies: "Seeing is no seeing." This is no answer, you might say. But it is a most perfect answer when it comes out of one's real inner experience. But when it is just in the form of words it loses its real sense. It is mere parrot's repetition, or mere echoing.

When seeing takes place in this wise, who is it that sees? If seeing is no seeing who is the seer. When the question was asked in this way the master said: "There is no seer either." When we use the word to see or to hear or to do we think there is a seer, one who hears, one who acts, and so on. But the master says there is no seer. There is no hearer. There is no ego. There is no *ātman* that acts, feels, thinks, and so on. But whenever we assume something, there comes along this bifurcation of subject and object. That is inevitable.

Now you will remember a question was asked when a master produced that stick and said: "If you say this stick is a stick, that is an assertion, if you say it is not a stick, that is a negation. Beyond this negation and affirmation, make a statement." What is this one statement which goes beyond negation and assertion?

There was another master who was asked for the one statement that goes beyond assertion and negation, and he replied: "What do *you* say?" That was the answer given to this question. I wonder what *you* make of this! When you make an absolute statement which goes beyond the duality of negation and affirmation, the master asks, "What do *you* say?" When you understand this you will understand everything.

Now when you are facing reality this point of thought is dangerous. When you actually see Godhead face to face you will lose your life. This is a question of life and death, and is therefore most dangerous. Yet in Zen you have to face this thought. Just stand in front of the thought and grasp it. When the master answered: "What would *you* do?" he just raised his thumb. To this serious question he gave just a trifling answer. The monk, of course, did not understand what the master said. Please be merciful, he said, and explain it. The master said: "Why, you're far off. You are no more at the point of the thought. You're just running away from it!"

"I come here with the most urgent question. Will you be good enough to solve it for me?" When that question was proposed to the master, the master simply said: "Do you understand?" The Monk wanted to understand; therefore, he questioned. But the master asked: "Do *you* understand?" Of course he did not understand; that is why he came with the question to the master. It is a most absurd answer from the ordinary point of view. Then the monk replied, quite naturally "I do not, oh master!" Then the master said: "The arrow has passed away." All these things are not to be intellectually treated.

There was another monk who came to a master and asked: "What is myself?" That is the most absolute question one can ever ask. What is myself? You must surely know yourself, yet instead of doing that you come to somebody else and ask, "What am I?" I ought to know myself far better than all of you combined. Even God himself cannot under-stand me as well as I myself. Yet we all ask this kind of question. Who am I?

And the master said: "How many masters have you asked about this question?" This kind of search may go on for ever, but Absolute Self is to be perceived within oneself.

# *Explaining Zen II*

In "Explaining Zen I" I talked about our wishing to go home—to go back to our original home, wherever it might be. Now in a well-known *mondo,* a dialogue between a monk and a Zen master, the monk asked the master: "What is Zen?" The Master said: "It is like seeking an ox while riding on it." Then the monk asked: "After I have ridden on the ox, what about it?" The master repeated, "It is like going home, while riding on the ox."

When Buddha attained Enlightenment he felt as if he had got home. He had found his own Self, the Self which he had had from the very beginning. But when he made an inquiry about it he lost it, for without losing it, without negating it, we cannot find it. It is of course unnecessary to try to find it if it has been with us from the very beginning, but the strange thing is that we have to lose it in order to find it, in order to be convinced that finding is not necessary at all. It is like the parable in the Bible of the prodigal son, who wanted to go home. In the *Saddharma Puṇḍarīka* we have the same theory of a son who ran away from his father's house, and after wandering about and going through all kinds of suffering, went back home. But the son was not able to identify himself as the heir to his father. He still thinks he is a stranger, and behaves as if he did not belong to his father. But the father, taking pity on him, uses all kinds of "expedients" or "methods" to make him feel at home. This story must have a common origin with that in the Bible, and this common origin may be traced back to our wishing for home—for we are all wanderers, wayfarers who have somehow lost our way.

Now when Christians deviate from the path which they are told by God to follow, this disobedience constitutes a sin, and because of this disobedience they feel the desire to be back in God. It is because they feel sinful that they wish to go back to God; it is the reminding themselves of their disobedience that makes them wish to go back to their original home. But the original home is never found unless we first go out of the home for once at least—that is, unless we commit some kind of sin.

Now this is very interesting. Why have we deviated? Why was it necessary to deviate from God—to run away from our original home? Why did we not stay with God? Why did we deny God? This question cannot be solved intellectually, however much we use our present logic. We have to develop another kind of logic which is not revealed through the exercise of the intellect. But as soon as this experience, that is, Enlightenment, is experienced, the question "why" has no force whatever; it solves itself. We are what we are. Because we are not in reality we ask the question "why," but as soon as we are in reality itself we no more ask that question. But we are troubled with the sense of sin. We have lost ourselves, and deviated from the course that the Buddha or God indicated. We are lost and want to be back home. How do we manage it? Zen does not extend a helpful hand to take us into Zen itself. Rather it stands before us as an "Iron Wall" which we cannot scale, which we cannot break through. We just face it and do not know what to do.

We try, as the Buddha did in the beginning, an intellectual way of breaking through the wall. In the Buddha's time the problem was in the form of the cycle of birth and death. Nowadays we may formulate it in a different way, but the fundamental problem remains the same. How to break through this wall of dualism? Without dualism we should not have this world. But we are in the world, and want to get out of the world. Why are we not satisfied with this world? Why do we wish to transcend the situation in which we find ourselves? From the intellectual point of view, from the scientific point of view, the situation is not of our own making. In Christian terminology, God made *us*. As long as we are God's creatures, the responsibility must be placed on God himself; it cannot be said that we are responsible for what we are. But somehow we feel that we *are* responsible for it, and want to get away from it, or at least to ameliorate it.

Now intellect cannot solve the problem. It only involves us more desperately in the labyrinth in which we find ourselves. Before the Buddha had his Enlightenment experience he tried this intellectual method. He followed the most noted philosophers of his day, but he could not find a solution through discussing the problem with them. Then he tried the practice of asceticism, that is, a moral discipline. He trained himself morally, by reducing his natural or physical impulses to the minimum, so that his mind or *ātman,* whatever you may call it, might be as free as possible. But this excess of discipline acted unfavorably on his health, and he became so emaciated that he could not rise from his seat. So he quit this method too, and began to take milk. But taking milk and getting stronger left the problem still unsolved, and it hung before his mind like a threatening thought. He could not make that thought his own; it remained outside himself and threatened him.

This is the situation which modern man feels in his own way. The words that the Buddha used to express his situation may be different, but the situation is the same. And it is threatening. Yet we have created this situation for ourselves and it is an illusion that the thought or problem is standing before us threatening us and demanding solution. There is no such thing, objectively speaking, outside the person who puts the question. The question is not threatening at all. It is the questioner who asks that question who is really threatening himself, and this threat comes in the form of the question. The situation, then, is that we are all suffering from an intellectual illusion which is nowadays known as logic or science. Scientists try to solve the secrets of existence by means of scientific research, but after they have—as they think— found the secret, that secret leads to another secret, and the secrets never cease. Those scientists who realize this, who know that the secrets are endless and that we can never grasp the infinite, think that there must be something beyond human measurement. For all those scientific secrets are measured by human measurement, and they at least appreciate that this human measurement must itself be solved. For the implement with which the average scientist attempts to measure other things, itself requires another implement to measure it. Yet there must be some way of solving the riddle, for moral discipline is no more efficient than the intellect. As long as morality strives to acquire something, to attain something—some kind of perfection—we realize, as soon as we attain a certain degree of moral discipline, that there is still something that we have not attained. So the perfection recedes for ever, for there is no such thing as perfection as far as human measurement is concerned. The intellectual approach and the moral approach are, therefore, alike—of no avail. Yet, because we have put the question that question is solvable.

The very fact that we have set forth a certain problem which we may call the ultimate question of reality proves that the question is solvable. There is no question which can never be answered, and we have in Zen the saying: "Questioning is answering." You do not ask in order to get an answer from others; you just look within to see who asked the question. This measurement—who produced that measure? Instead of trying to evaluate a ruler by another ruler we return to the One who created the ruler itself. In theological terminology, we might say that as God created the world why not go to God himself? Instead of bothering with the created, why not go directly to the Creator? When God said, "Let there be light," the world came out. But where from? There is nowhere else but from God himself. In that case the world must have God in itself. God must be present in the world. If he stayed outside the world, if God stands against the world and the world against God, the world is no more a living world, and God is a dead machine. If God was able to create the world, the world must have something of God in it. In the same way, if we ask a question something of the answer that produced that question must be in us. So the solution of a problem takes place when question and questioner become one, that is when God and the world become one. When God created the world, that was God's question. God, by creating the world questioned himself. He wanted to know himself. When God created the world, he solved his question, and when he identified himself with the world, when the world was identified with God, the complete solution took place. God created the world out of himself; therefore, to solve the problem of the world God has to go back into himself. When this takes place God understands himself. Therefore God negates himself when he wants to know himself.

At the same time we want to go back to our original home where no negations, no affirmations ever existed, and no logic could ever apply. But if we seek that original home outside the world, and that original home is lost in the world itself, we shall have to seek another original home. So the original home must be in the world out of which the original home comes; that is, God must be in the world. Therefore, when the world is known, God is known, and when God is known, the world is known. This identification must take place before the final answer takes place.

So when the Buddha became enlightened, in his Enlightenment experience there was no question standing outside him, no questioner who produced that question. So the question dissolved itself into the question out of which the question came. And the questioner took the question into himself. When this identification took place the Buddha solved his question. Thereafter, his experience could not be demonstrated in any way except by saying "Oh," or "Ah," or "*Om,*" or some such monosyllable which makes no articulate sense. In Zen teaching, words are therefore not used in the way they are generally used, for they have no relative sense. They all come out of the experience itself. Theologians say: "Believe first and you will be saved. Do not question about it, just believe it, and by believing you will be saved." But this believing is itself what those who have not attained faith are looking for. When faith is attained everything solves itself. But how to get that faith, that is the question, and we all ask it.

When we are told, "Believe and you will be saved," how to believe is the question, for faith is not a thing that comes from outside. Faith is what the Buddha experienced at the time of Enlightenment. Questioner and question must become one. When this one-ness is experienced, that is the state of faith.

Then what is faith and how can I be saved? As long as that question lingers outside oneself it will never be solved; that is, there will be no faith. Therefore, having faith is being saved, and being saved is having faith. Faith and salvation take place simultaneously. Faith *is* being saved; being saved is faith. So we must have faith first; otherwise, there will be no solution.

When psychology is used in its scientific or relative aspect it is just one of the sciences and will not apply to the Buddha's Enlightenment experience. But when it is understood in its broadest and deepest possible sense, the Zen approach to it concerns the *Ātman* or Self. But whether we talk of Self or Reality the main thing is to experience it, and experience concerns the Will. Now we *are* will, and God is will, and when will asserts itself, not in its relative sense of a craving for power but in its original sense, we may speak of God's will.

God wills to know himself, and this will, that is, God, moves, for God can never stand still. God moves and this movement is will. So what moves movement, what starts movement, is will. When God remains just as God, there is no world, there is indeed no God. Then God wills and when this motion or movement takes place, creation takes place. Each time I move my finger, the world is created. This is God's creation. Each time I utter a word this utterance is God's fiat. And this is will. To start from this will, to know what this will is, this is the psychological approach to Zen.

Now Eckhart has much to say about the saying, "Blessed are the poor in spirit," which is the most illuminating statement in the Bible. What does "poor" mean here, asks Eckhart. He replies: "The poor man, the one who is poor, is the one who wants nothing, knows nothing and has nothing. This exactly corresponds to the Zen idea."

"*Wants nothing*" means having no desire. When I said God wills, and that something comes out of the willing, it is already misstating reality as it is. But when we try to express reality in language, this contradiction and absurdity is inevitable. So I say that Will wills without willing or wanting anything. If God wills to create the world, something outside of himself, that kind of Will is no will. The divine will is just Will, and out of it the world comes. So God willed to create the world, as if he did not will at all. That's what Eckhart means by the poor man.

"*Knows nothing*" is another most expressive phrase. When we try to know something there is one who wants to know and something which is to be known; there is dichotomy. But God's knowing is not knowing at all.

And then there is "*not to have.*" Eckhart says that if there is any one spot in the soul, however small, where God could be placed, God will never come into your soul. God does not want any place or point where he could set himself up. Within such a place you are God himself.

Of this *wanting nothing* he gives a fine example. Pious people continue their penances and external practices of piety, and are popularly considered of great importance. But Eckhart says "May God pardon it"! To all outward appearance these people are to be called holy, but inwardly they are fools, for they do not understand the true meaning of divine reality. By practicing penances, by looking virtuous, by saying prayers and attending Mass, and so on, they are quite religious people. But if they want something, if they are seeking something, they are really fools.

Compare this with the question of a Zen master: "Who is the teacher of all patriarchs?" or, we might say, all church fathers? His own answer was, "Cows and dogs." We think these are inferior to us, and this delusion troubles us all the time. The cat catches rats, and in that, the cat is performing his cat-ness. So long as he performs his cat-ness, he is divine. But we human beings deviate from the original nature which God intended us to have, and in that we are worse than cats, and we have something to learn from them.

There is another story. A monk asked a Zen master: "Everybody is supposed to have Buddha-nature. Have I got it?" The master replied, "No." Then the monk asked: "When the Buddhist scriptures tell us that everything is endowed with Buddha-nature, how is it that I don't have it? Trees and rocks, rivers and mountains, all have Buddha-nature. If so, why not I!" The master replied, "Cats, dogs, mountains, rivers, all have Buddha-nature; you do not." The monk asked, "Why not?" The master said: "Because you ask!"

But if we do not ask, how do we know it? That is the quandary. Eckhart says, do not want anything. Then he talks of *knowing*. Do not, he says, try to know anything. Each time I read Eckhart's sermons it strikes me how identical his thought is with Zen teaching, or with my own experience, I might say.

Back in the womb from which I came I had no God, and merely was myself. I did not will or desire anything. For I was pure being and knower of myself by divine truth. Then I wanted myself and nothing else. And what I wanted was, and what I was I wanted. And thus I existed untrammeled by God or anything else. But when I parted from my free will and received my created being then I had a God. For before there were creatures God was not God, but rather he was what he was. When creatures came to be and took on creaturely being, then God was no longer God, as he is in himself, but God as he is with creatures.

On the question of not knowing anything, he says: "Now the question is raised—in what does happiness consist most of all? Certain authorities have said that it consists in *loving*. Love is what constitutes happiness. Others say that it consists in *knowing* and *loving*. And this is a better statement."

But Eckhart says that happiness consists neither in knowledge nor in love, but that there is something in the soul from which both knowledge and love flow. To know this source from which love and knowledge flow is to know what blessedness depends on. This something has no before or after. It waits for nothing that is yet to come; it has nothing to gain or lose. Thus, when God acts in it, it is deprived of knowing that he has done so. So this kind of knowledge is not knowing anything.

The last of Eckhart's attributes of the poor man was not to have anything. There was a monk who studied Zen under a certain master. He took down every word the master said just as modern students do, and he kept his notebooks. One day the master called him in. "Now that you have been with me so many years you must know something about Zen. Tell me what you understand. So the monk said what he thought he understood, but the master did not accept his understanding. Whatever statement he made the master denied. He was so grieved, because he thought he understood Zen, that he went back to his own room and went over his notebook, page after page, trying to find a suitable word which would satisfy the master; but he could not find one. He was so disappointed that he thought it was not in him to understand Zen. So he departed from the master, and decided to devote himself to doing something pious. He went to a famous Zen master's grave and devoted himself to keeping the tombstone clean and the surrounding lawn well swept and in good order. One day, when he was cleaning around the tomb, he accidentally struck his bamboo broom against a stone. The striking caused a certain sound, and when he heard that he instantly understood all that his master had said, saying, "Last year my poverty" (note how this corresponds to Eckhart's idea of poverty) "was something like the point of a drill, a very small point. My poverty was such that I had nothing but the small point of the drill. This year my poverty is such that there is no drill, and there is no ground in which its point could be inserted. So I am entirely poor." This corresponds to what Eckhart means, for if there is any spot left in one's mind or soul God will never come in there; Christ will never be born in that soul. The mind must be entirely empty of the things we generally put into it. When this takes place there is real God, that is, real poverty—not to want anything, not to know anything, not to have anything.

Here is another story about not knowing. There was a master who studied Zen under another master, and he was noted for his understanding of Zen. There was a monk who came to that master whose name was Sekito, and the monk knew very well that he was a great master. But just to try how much he understood the monk proposed this question: "Eno, your master, taught you the Dharma, and you have taught many others. Do you understand that Dharma?"

Now everybody knew that Sekito was a great master, with perfect understanding of the Dharma taught by Eno, his predecessor, and the monk knew it too. Yet he purposely asked this question. Sekito replied, "I do not understand the Dharma." If he pretended to know something there would at once be knower and known. So not knowing—transcending this dichotomy of subject-object—is really to be in this dichotomy itself.

Another interesting remark which Eckhart makes is this: "If anyone does not understand this discourse let him not worry about that. For if he does not find this truth in himself, he cannot understand what I have said. For it is the discovered truth which comes immediately from the heart of God."

[Asked about the relationship between asceticism and Zen, Dr. Suzuki replied:] This is a point which invites misunderstanding. To understand Zen, asceticism is not needed; intellectual acuteness is not needed. If asceticism is practiced without any connection with attaining Enlightenment, this is all right. To discipline oneself in something, asceticism may be needed. But to try to reach Enlightenment by means of asceticism is wrong. That does not condemn asceticism, as ascetic discipline of the body or mind, but this distinction is most strongly to be made. The same with intellectuality. Zen experience itself needs some expression, and the experience, if it is a genuine experience, expresses itself. When it expresses itself it generally goes through the channel of intellection, but to attempt to reach Zen from the intellectual point of view is difficult, if not impossible.

# *The Supreme Spiritual Ideal*

In July, 1936, Sir Francis Younghusband convened in London a World Congress of Faiths which, in a fortnight's hard work of discussions, punctuated by public meetings and ensuing questions, hammered out, with remarkable goodwill, the common ground of some seven religions.

At the Queen's Hall on July 9th, one of the speakers was Dr. D. T. Suzuki, and many who later discussed with me that memorable evening made the same remark, that all they remembered was his speech. The theme was no less than The Supreme Spiritual Ideal, and this would not do for a master of Zen with little liking for generalities. As I noted in my diary at the time, "he seemed to be dozing when roused by the Chairman for his contribution. Then with his soft and gentle voice he reached up, as it were, and brought the subject down to earth, where the heart may understand it and the hands make use of it." Here it is, taken from a large volume of the proceedings published by Watkins in 1937 as *Faiths and Fellowship* and republished by courtesy of the present Society in Norfolk Square—ED.

When I was first asked to talk about the Supreme Spiritual Ideal I did not exactly know what to answer. Firstly, I am just a simple-minded country-man from a far-away corner of the world suddenly thrust into the midst of this hustling city of London, and I am bewildered and my mind refuses to work in the same way that it does when I am in my own land. Secondly, how can a humble person like myself talk about such a grand thing as the Supreme Spiritual Ideal, and this before such a grand assembly of people, everyone of whom looks to me to be so wise and intelligent, knowing everything that is under the sun? I am ashamed that I have somehow been made to stand here. The first mistake was committed when I left Japan.

Let me tell you how I lived before I came to London. In my country we have straw-thatched houses. Japanese houses are mostly little. Well, still in the country you see many such straw houses, and mine is one of them. I get up in the morning with the chirping of the birds. I open windows which look right into the garden. Japanese windows are quite different from your English windows. English windows are somewhat like holes made in the walls, but Japanese windows are a combination of English windows and walls. So when Japanese windows are opened, one side of the house is entirely taken away. The house itself opens right into the garden. There is no division between the house and the garden. The garden is a house, a house is a garden; but here a house is quite separate. A house stands by itself, and so does its occupant. Its occupant is separated from his or her surroundings altogether. There is nature, here I am; you are you, I am I; so there does not seem to be any connection between those two—nature, natural surroundings, and the occupants of the house.

So by opening Japanese windows, the house continues into the garden. And I can look at the trees quite easily, not as I look from the English window—that is a kind of peeping out into the garden. I just see the trees growing from the ground. And when I look at those trees growing right from the ground, I seem to feel something mysterious which comes from the trees and from the mother earth herself. And I seem to be living with them, and they in me and with me. I do not know whether this communion could be called spiritual or not. I have no time to call it anything, I am just satisfied. Then there is the little pond, a little lower down the garden. I hear the fish occasionally leaping out of the pond as though they were altogether too happy, and could not stay contented swimming in the pond. Are they? I do not know, but I somehow feel they are very very happy indeed. Just as we dance when we are filled with joy, so the fish are surely dancing. Do they also get something from the element in which they live and have their being? What is this something, after all, which seems to be so stirred in my own self, as I listen to the dancing of the fish in the pond?

Then this is the time for the lotuses to bloom. The pond is filled with them, and my imagination travels far out to the other end of the globe. When I talk like this, do you think I am dreaming in the middle of this big city? Perhaps I am. But my dream, I feel somehow, is not altogether an idle one. Could not there be in these things of which I am dreaming something of eternal and universal value? These huge buildings I see about me are really grand work, grand human achievements, no doubt.

I had a similar feeling when I visited China and was confronted with the Great Wall, of which you have perhaps heard. Are they, however, of eternal duration, as I like to say my dreams are? Let the earth shake a little. Here in this part of the earth, fortunately, it does not seem to shake so frequently as it does in Japan. But let it shake for once. Well, I wonder what would be the result? I can see that result. I even refuse to think of it. But some time ago in an American magazine a certain writer wrote about the ruins of the city of New York when possible future explorers will try to locate where certain of the highest buildings in the world—they call them skyscrapers, don't they—which are now standing in New York would have been. But I will not go on any more with this kind of talk; I must stop dreaming, though it is very pleasant.

Let me awake and face actualities. But what are those actualities I am facing now?—not you, not this building, not the microphone, but this Supreme Spiritual Ideal, those high-sounding words. They come from me. I can't be any longer dreaming of anything. I must make my mind come back to this subject, the Supreme Spiritual Ideal. But really I do not know what Spiritual is, what Ideal is, what Supreme Spiritual Ideal is. I do not seem to be able to comprehend exactly the true significance of these three words, placed so conspicuously before me.

Here in London I come out of the hotel where I am staying. I see in the streets so many men and women walking—or rather, running hurriedly, for to my mind they don't seem to be walking; they seem to be really running. It may not be quite correct to say so, but it seems to me so. And then their expressions are more or less strained, their facial muscles are contracted intensely; they could be more easily relaxed. The roads are riddled with all kinds of vehicles, buses, cars, and other things; they seem to be running in a constant stream—in a constant, ceaseless stream—and I don't know when I can step into that constantly flowing stream of vehicles. The shops are decorated with all kinds of things, most of which I don't seem to need in my little straw-thatched house. When I see all these things, I cannot help wondering where the so-called modern civilized people are ultimately going. What is their destiny? Are they in the pursuit of the Supreme Spiritual Ideal? Are their intense expressions somehow symbolic of their willingness to look into the spirituality of things? Are they really going to spread this spirituality into the farthest end of the globe? I do not know. I cannot answer.

Now let me see, spirituality is generally contrasted to the material, ideal to actual or practical, and supreme to commonplace. If when we talk about the Supreme Spiritual Ideal, does it really mean to do away with what seems to be material, not idealistic but practical and prosaic, not supreme but quite commonplace—this our everyday life in this big city? When we talk about spirituality, do we have to do away with all these things? Does spirituality signify something quite apart from what we see around here? I do not think this way of talking, dividing spirit from matter and matter from spirit, a very profitable way of looking at things about us. As to this dualistic interpretation of reality as matter and spirit, I made some references to it in my little speech the other day.

In point of fact, matter and spirit are one, or rather, they represent two sides of one reality. The wise will try to take hold of the reality, the shield itself, instead of just looking at this side or that side of it, known sometimes as matter and sometimes as spirit. For when the material side alone is taken hold of, there will be nothing spiritual in matter. When the spiritual side alone is emphasized, matter will have to be altogether ignored. The result in either case is onesidedness, the crippling of reality, which ought to be kept whole and wholesome, too. When our minds are properly adjusted and are able to grasp the reality which is neither spirit nor matter and yet which is, of course, spirit and matter, I venture to say that with all its materiality London is supremely spiritual; and further, when our minds are crookedly adjusted, all the monasteries and temples, all the cathedrals and all the ecclesiastic orders in connection with them, all the holy places with their holy paraphernalia, with all their devout worshippers, with everything that goes in the name of religion, I venture to say again are nothing but materiality, heaps of dirt, sinks of corruption.

To my mind, the material is not to be despised, and the spiritual is not always to be exalted—I mean anything which goes in the name of spiritual; I do not mean anything that is really spiritual, but things that pride themselves on the name of spiritual. Such things are not always to be exalted. Those who talk about spirituality are sometimes men of violent nature, while amongst those who have amassed large fortunes and seem ever to be inclined towards things material we often find the highest and biggest souls, stepped in spirituality. But the main difficulty is how can I bring my straw-thatched house right into the midst of these solidly built-up London walls? And how can I construct my humble hut right in the midst of this Oxford Circus? How can I do that in the confusion of cars, buses, and all kinds of conveyances? How can I listen to the singing of the birds, and also to the leaping of the fish? How can one turn all the showings of the shop window displays into the freshness of the green leaves swayed by the morning breeze? How am I to find the naturalness, artlessness, utter self-abandonment of nature in the utmost artificiality of human works? This is the great problem set before us these days.

Again, I do not know about the Supreme Spiritual Ideal. But as I am forced to face this so-called materiality of modern civilization, I have to make some comments on it. As long as man is the work of nature and even the work of God, what he does, what he makes, cannot altogether be despised as material and contrasted to the so-called spiritual. Somehow it must be material-spiritual or spiritual-material, with the hyphen between these two terms—spiritual not divided from material, material not severed from spiritual, but both combined, as we read, with a hyphen. I do not like to make references to such concepts as objectivity and subjectivity, but for lack of a suitable term, just at this moment let me say this. If the spiritual-material, linked with a hyphen, cannot be found objectively, let us find it in our subjective minds and work it out so as to transform the entire world in accordance with it.

Let me tell you how this was worked out by an ancient master. His name was Yoshu, and the monastery in which he used to live was noted for its natural stone bridge. Monasteries are generally built in the mountains, and this place where Yoshu used to reside was noted for its stone bridge over the rapids. One day a monk came to the master and asked: "This place is very well-known for its natural stone bridge, but as I come here I don't see any stone bridge. I just see a rotten piece of board, a plank. Where is your bridge, pray tell me, O master?" That was a question given to the master, and the master now answered this way: "You only see that miserable, rickety plan and don't see the stone bridge?" The disciple said: "Where is the stone bridge then?" And this is the master's answer: "Horses pass over it, donkeys pass over it, cats and dogs. . . ." (Excuse me if I add a little more than the master actually said.) "Cats and dogs, tigers and elephants pass over it, men and women, the poor and the rich, the young and the old, the humble and the noble (any amount of those opposites might be enumerated);

Englishmen, perhaps Japanese, Muslims, Christians; spirituality and materiality, the ideal and the practical, the supreme and the most commonplace things. They all pass over it, even you, O monk, who refuse to see it, are really walking over it quite nonchalantly; and above all you are not thankful for it at all. You don't say, 'I thank you' for crossing over the bridge. What good is this stone bridge then? Do we see it? Are we walking on it? The bridge does not cry out and say: 'I am your supreme spiritual ideal.' The stone bridge lies flat and goes on silently from the beginningless past perhaps to the endless future."

I must stop here. Thank you for your kind attention to my Japanese English. I expect you have done your best to understand me. Then the kindness must be mutual, and in this mutuality of kindness, do we not seize a little glimpse of what we call Spiritual World Fellowship?

Dr. Suzuki, Christmas Humphreys, and Dr. Edward Conze outside the premises of The Buddhist Society in London, 1958.

Mr. G. Koizumi, Founder of the Budokwai in London, with Dr. Suzuki in the garden of Mr. and Mrs. Christmas Humphreys in London, 1958.

# Index

115

, identification
seeing

, intuition

22. Prajñā- transcendental wisdom or ≡ enlightenment
   └ not knowing but knowing & seeing (subject & object)

6. Dharmakaya - eternal motherhood. Essence - body,
Being-body, Suchness, Conceived by the human
heart as love & wisdom. The source of infinite.
love the good he does is not for his own interest; the evil he avoids
   / a doctrine complementary to karma "not for his own benefit"
9 - Parinamana   "vicarious sacrifice" - to sacrifice
one's interests for the benefit of others. Conceived
in its cosmic aspect rather than individually.
(Derives its sanction directly from the human heart.
· emphasizes the universal or supra-individual
signific. of karma.
also, the promotion of goodness, the annihilation of
"thee" & "me", the recognition of oneness of all
                                                    of things.

   ┌ is terrible
Karma-(p 11), inflexible law of nature, irreconcileable,
is most rigidly masculine & knows no mercy
                                    1. Parinamana is
humane, most tenderly feminine, always ready
to weep & help.